HEALED IN THE NAME OF JESUS
Keep Your Faith in God's Healing Promises

Jonathan Srock

If you enjoy this book, please subscribe to my website.

Signing up gives you a free gift

and updates to my writings and ministry activity.

Go to www.Jonathansrock.com

Thank you for your support!

Other Books by Jonathan Srock

Holiness Matters: A Call to Obey the Holy Spirit

A Short Guide to Sharing Your Faith

The Passion Chronicles: the Last Week of Jesus' Life

The Greatest Gift Series: 12 Lives Changed by Jesus' Birth

Healed in the Name of Jesus:
Keep Your Faith in God's Healing Promises

Jonathan Srock

Foreword by
Pastor Wayne Schaeffer

HEALED IN THE NAME OF JESUS: KEEP YOUR FAITH IN GOD'S HEALING PROMISES

Copyright © 2022 by Jonathan Srock. All rights reserved. Except for brief quotations in critical publications or reviews, no part of this book may be reproduced in any manner without prior written permission from the publisher. Write: Permissions. Jonathan Srock, 87 Safe Harbor Ln., Smithmill, PA 16680

Jonathan Srock
87 Safe Harbor Ln.
Smithmill, PA 16680
https://www.Jonathansrock.com

ISBN 13: 978-1-63972-288-4

Cataloguing-in-Publication Data

Healed in the Name of Jesus: Keep Your Faith in God's Healing Promises by Jonathan Srock; foreword by Wayne Schaeffer.

iv + 217 p.; 23 cm. Includes bibliographical references.
ISBN 13: 978-1-63972-288-4
I. Srock, Jonathan. Foreword Schaeffer, Wayne.
III. Healed in the Name of Jesus: Keep Your Faith in God's Healing Promises.

CALL NUMBER 2022

Manufactured in the U.S.A.   2022

All Scripture quotations noted are my own translations. All rights reserved..

Edited by Lois E. Olena

Cover Design: Alabi Gbenga Emmanuel, Website: www.fiverr.com/emmsdigital

Dedication

To every Christian who suffers

an affliction and waits for your physical healing,

never stop believing that God's promises

are yes and amen

Contents

Foreword iii

Acknowledgments iv

Introduction "God Hasn't Healed Me … Yet." 1

Chapter 1 Acknowledge Your Affliction 15

Chapter 2 Believe God's Promises 35

Chapter 3 Pray for Your Healing 55

Chapter 4 Trust through Dark Times 77

Chapter 5 Wait for Your Healing 95

Chapter 6 Demolish Your Doubt 115

Chapter 7 Minister in Your Affliction 137

Chapter 8 Step toward Your Healing 157

Chapter 9 Be Encouraged for Your Healing 179

Chapter 10 Minister to the Afflicted 201

Dear Reader 215

About the Author 217

Foreword

Jonathan asked me to write a foreword for this book before Jonathan completed it. Having now read through it, I would have gladly volunteered to do so. I want to encourage you to read what Jonathan Srock has written on the subject matter of being Healed in the Name of Jesus. Through his own personal journey and biblical insight, Jonathan gives a realistic picture of the serious nature of divine healing.

From Jonathan's tragic paralysis to the promises of God's healing, this book will discuss various spiritual disciplines that have become a staple in his personal life. Jonathan teaches the doctrine of divine healing throughout this book. From acknowledging your sickness to praying and trusting the Lord for your healing, to how to pray for others in the midst of your own affliction.

There is a fire that burns within Jonathan's life to see people saved and healed in Jesus' name. Having served many years as a pastor, you will find the heart of a shepherd in the words of this book. As you read it, you will feel as if you are having a conversation with him. You will get wisdom, experience, humor, and practical advice without the hype or exaggeration. Jonathan brings humility and honesty to the discussion on divine healing and much more.

So I am grateful to introduce you to a book you will treasure. Don't just read the book. Pull out your highlighter and mark it up. Use it to take you onward in your faith, hope, and belief that God is able to heal through the work of Jesus Christ.

For me, the ministry has almost always been a joy. I have never thought of it as a job. Yet one of the greatest challenges has always been having the faith to pray for and believe in God for miraculous healing. Have I seen them in my 30 years of ministry? Yes. Do I understand why some are healed and others aren't? No. I am thankful for pastors like Jonathan Srock who are able to inspire us to trust and obey, then let God do the rest.

So, sit down with this book like you would sit down with a friend, and glean a wealth of godly wisdom. Be encouraged that God is able.

News about him spread all over Syria, and people brought to him all who were ill with various diseases, those suffering severe pain, the demon-possessed, those having seizures, and the paralyzed; and he healed them (Matthew 4:24 NIV).

Wayne Schaeffer
Presbyter South Central West Section of the Penn-Del Ministry Network
Lead Pastor of New Life Worship Center
Altoona, Pennsylvania

Acknowledgments

Writing a book is one of the hardest accomplishments to achieve. Many people want to write a book, but few come so far as to publish a work after slaving over it for months, even years. This book is not only my accomplishment, but brought to fruition because of the professionals and friends who have helped me make it the very best ministry tool for the afflicted as possible.

To that end, I want to thank as many people as I can remember have helped me in some way to make this book possible. If I forget any of them, my deepest apologies. I wish to give credit where credit is due.

I want to thank God for all the gifts He has given me to write this book. As a sufferer of paralysis until His healing, I want to use my experience to help others in similar circumstances. My parents have not only brought me up in the ways of the Lord and provided a godly example to me, but they have also been involved in the background of this book. They have encouraged me, read and edited some of this manuscript, and are my caregivers when nurses cannot be here.

I thank my nurses, who probably do not want their names published in this book. They know who they are. A couple of them have read this book and helped me with the medical terminology in it. But they have done much more than that. They care for me on a daily basis. They rarely call off work. Each nurse has braved harrowing weather in the winter and some storms. They are faithful, and I am blessed that each one of them is in my life.

Thank you to Pastor Wayne Schaeffer, my presbyter, for taking the time and effort to write the Foreword for this book. He has known me since I was a teenager. He has watched me all these years, and now supports me in my ministry endeavors. He is a blessing to myself, our section, and our district.

I also want to thank my amazing editor. Lois Olena is one of the best editors I could ever imagine. Her thorough approach, thoughtful questions, helpful organization and formatting, astute theological knowledge, and kindness have benefited me through a couple of books. I wouldn't hesitate to ask for her services again.

The youth pastor at my church, Cal McIntosh took time out of his busy schedule to take professional pictures of me that were used in this book and are used throughout my website and ministry. I also want to thank my book cover designer, Alabi Gbenga Emmanuel for designing an incredibly beautiful and professional book cover for all formats of the book. He worked tirelessly with me to come up with a design that fits this book and its subject of divine healing.

This book has the advantage of being read and vetted by many beta readers. They have given their time and understanding to reading every word in this book. I can't thank them enough for their time and effort in previewing this book and giving me great suggestions on how to improve it before publication. The beta readers who have contributed to this book are Pastor Wayne Schaeffer, Pastor Marvin Nemitz, Ryan Grabill, Immer Lopez, Pastors Zac and Ashley McDonald, Mark and Betsy Frailey, Pastor Nate Yocum, Dawn Elizabeth, Pastor Pete Kramer, Pastor Ella Kerstetter, Ruth Noel, Scott and Magevney Strickland, Carole Wise, Pastor Jonathan and Lisa Hendren, Pastor Tom Rees, Anna Holloway, and many others.

Finally, I want to thank my book launch team who have helped me after publication with marketing and promoting this book. I believe God had me write this book for those who suffer afflictions and struggle with keeping their faith in God's promises. But most people will never hear of the book without the help of my book launch team. They help me let people know that this book exists. I personally want to thank all my beta readers who have promoted my book as book launchers as well.

Introduction
"God Hasn't Healed Me ... Yet."

> "I am convinced of this: the one who began a good work in you will complete it until the day of Christ Jesus" (Philippians 1:6).

When you suffer an illness or disorder, it challenges your faith in God's promises. When trials challenge your hope and faith, that does not necessarily mean you are doubting. You just need faith warriors to come alongside you and encourage you. As I tell my story, I want to be one of those warriors with you.

In this book, we will fight the battle for our trust in God's healing promises together. Are you in the middle of an impossible medical situation? Have doctors and medical professionals told you they can't do anything for you? I live in that space. Since 2013, I have been paralyzed from the neck down.

As a minister of the gospel, I still struggle to maintain my faith in God's healing promises when my reality opposes the fulfillment of those promises for me. I want to join you in the battle. Let us fight together to keep our faith until the fulfillment of what God has promised us.

This is My Story

That day began like any other. It was one of my favorite days of the week—Wednesday—which I spent preparing for our evening Bible study at the church I had become pastor of four years before.

I love diving into God's Word and discovering diamonds to share with others. I learn more when I research and teach the Bible. I had jumped in the shower to enjoy a hot, awakening experience. Suddenly, my fingers on both hands closed, and my thumbs stuck straight out.

It is impossible to open your fingers when they won't cooperate. I was, quite literally, *all thumbs*! Sensing something was very wrong, I got out of the shower and tried to dry myself off. By the time I walked into my adjacent bedroom, I could not wiggle my toes or feel my feet. So, I grabbed my phone with both hands, laid across my bed, and covered myself up with the clothes I had laid out that morning.

I was quickly losing the ability to feel my arms and legs. I voice-dialed one of my deacons. The conversation made it sound like a prank call. "Lucy, are you busy right now?"

"Not yet, Pastor. Can I help you?"

"Yeah. This is not a joke. I believe I'm becoming paralyzed. I can't feel my arms or legs right now. I don't know what is going on. Can you come unlock the door of the parsonage for the paramedics? Oh, I didn't call any paramedics."

As the pastor of a smaller church, I was more concerned about how much it would cost to fix the door than with calling 911. I wasn't thinking clearly. All of this was new to me. I didn't know what was going on.

"Are you sure this isn't a joke?"

I think Lucy heard the panic in my voice. "No. It's no joke. If you can't make it, I don't know if I will. And since it's becoming harder to breathe and talk, I don't think I can call anyone else."

Thank God Lucy took me seriously. "OK, Pastor. I'll be right there!" I listened to the three beeps signaling that she had hung up. Time was running out.

I had never thought about my mortality until that moment. It dawned on me that I might not be alive by the time she arrived or got help. It's one thing to say you believe that God has your life in His hands. It's another to stand at death's door and try to trust Him with your life.

> "Jesus, whether I live or die, it's for your glory."

I laid there feeling the ability to move drain from my body. I tried to distract myself from the fear of my new reality. As my breathing became labored, I prayed a simple prayer: "Jesus, whether I live or die, it's for your glory."

I looked at my ceiling for the last time, closed my eyes, and passed out. I don't remember anything after that. Within thirty minutes of my fingers closing in the shower to the moment I closed my eyes, I was completely paralyzed.

For Those Who Need Faith

Are you suffering an incurable or terminal illness? Is some kind of sickness, disorder, injury, or other ailment taking control of each day of your life? I write this book for those who suffer long-term, incurable, or terminal conditions that science has deemed impossible to cure. Since that day in September 2013 when I was paralyzed from the neck down, I have lived every day believing God for total healing and declaring it over myself.

I am an Assemblies of God ordained minister. I have believed and preached God's promises for healing all my life. Since that day especially, I have had to put my faith where my mouth is. I still believe—now even more than before. As I tell you *my* story, look for how the message about my situation will apply to *you*.

How do we keep our faith in God's healing promises when we have not yet seen them fulfilled in our bodies? Join me as I tell you about my struggles and victories with paralysis while keeping my faith in Jesus's healing promises.

I'm not perfect. Like you, I have good and bad days. But I believe that for all of us, God has healing in store.

> In one sentence, I acknowledge my reality and assert my faith.

I don't write this book as a minister not suffering affliction, telling you to *just believe* in God's healing promises. I suffer my affliction even as I write this book. I speak not from the prospect of being healed already. I fight the battle of faith alongside you. I wait for my healing as you do.

We must trust God even though we have not yet seen our healing. Stay the course, and watch God finish His promised work in you. In the meantime, I share my story and my confidence in Jesus to do what He has promised in me. Let it serve as another testimony of faith in Jesus's power and in Him.

Relying on God for Healing

What do you focus on when I say, "God hasn't healed me yet?" Most people focus on the phrase, "God hasn't healed me" and rebuke me for saying that. But faith comes with that three-letter word at the end—*yet*. In one sentence, I acknowledge my reality and assert my faith.

When taken as a whole, this sentence does everything the afflicted did when they came to Jesus. They acknowledged their affliction, and Jesus healed them. They had faith because they came to Jesus. When I say, "Yet," I'm not saying that I don't believe God will heal me. I'm saying that I'm trusting Him to do it.

Saying, "God hasn't healed me yet" acknowledges the reality of my affliction now. But I trust God to change my reality in the future. With faith, I look forward to the day He heals me. My reality has not yet matched the fulfillment of God's healing promises for me. He's not done with your story, either.

Between God's Promise and Fulfillment

Like many saints, we live between God's promise for healing and its fulfillment in us. In this middle space between promise and fulfillment, we walk in a waiting period. We cannot heal ourselves. We must wait for God to finish His work in us.

The Bible outlines this time that we must wait for God to work His promise in us. As Abraham and Sarah waited for God to bring Isaac into the world, so we also wait for God to fulfill His promises in us. His promises are sure. He has never let us down or failed to bring His promises to completion.

But between God's promise and its fulfillment, we can lose hope and faith. We don't see the end from the beginning as He does. As we struggle in the battle and lose sight of the promise, we need believing warriors to come alongside us and lift our weary arms as Aaron and Hur held up Moses's hands (Exod 17:11-13).

We live in this gap since we are only human. We cannot see God's purpose in our suffering. With every ache and pain, we cry out in desperation for God. We ask *why*, and like Job, we don't always get an answer. We understand what God's Word says. We believe with our heads, but it's hard to transfer that knowledge to our hearts.

Our setbacks challenge our trust in God's promises. Even worse, they may challenge our faith in God. We either overcome our trials, or they overcome our trust. In this battle for victory over our affliction, we must stand strong and declare God's victory—even though we have not seen it yet.

> We either overcome our trials,
> or they overcome our trust.

Our faith goes before us. It sees the future God promises. We must let our faith lead us. In the middle of our affliction, we cannot see the end. We lose our way, and hope dwindles. If we do not maintain our faith, darkness will overtake us. In this space, we must double down on our faith and hope in God's promises. He has never failed us, and He will come through again. Let me encourage you to keep the faith in the middle of the storm.

God Heals by His Prerogative

My aim is to encourage you for divine physical healing. But God heals other wounds. I mention them here to show the greatness of our God.

Spiritual, Mental and Emotional Healing

We must not discredit the healing God does deep in our souls. Perhaps people might discount such healing because it is not outwardly noticeable.

When God heals us spiritually, we call it salvation. This involves more than saving us from death and hell. God resurrects our dead spirit. This amazing miracle of resurrection is the first step in salvation.

After spiritually raising us from the dead, God enlivens our spirits to His gospel—the good news that we can live forever as God designed us to do. This has come about through the death of His Son on the Cross and His resurrection out of the tomb. Jesus died so we can live eternally. Salvation continues as God molds us into the image of His Son.

> Some wounds may not be visible, but they still require God's healing.

These things are the beginning of spiritual healing. Many Christians have emotional, relational, and spiritual scars that need God's healing touch beyond salvation. Our brokenness plays out in our decisions, our relationships, and the course of our lives. Some wounds may not be visible, but they still require God's healing.

Jesus sees how deeply we hide from others. He knows the depths of pain and hurt in us. His healing of these invisible wounds feels as good as when He heals our bodies. We need His complete healing—body, mind, and spirit. His miracle working power for inner healing is no less important than physical healing.

Jesus's ultimate sacrifice demolishes every disease. God cures every ailment known to humanity in the shadow of the Cross. So, even more amazing than God's desire to heal our bodies is His desire for our mental health. Mental illness is real. This illness, too, stems from the fallen state of this world, from our broken environment, and from our diminishing temporal bodies. But Jesus sympathizes with our pain, suffering, and weaknesses (Heb 4:15). He sees all, knows all, and heals all. Nothing is so far gone that God cannot heal it. He created our bodies and is more than able to heal every wound and make us whole.

Natural Healing

Medical professionals attest to God's miraculous creation of the human body. God designed this mortal tent of ours with flawless creativity and forethought. Our bodies can heal many injuries naturally. Without a visit to a hospital or emergency room, many cuts and bruises will heal with time because He created our bodies with an immune system that can heal colds, fevers, and several other diseases. Think about the amazing creativity of our God! He protects our bodies against the dangers of this fallen world.

But this book is not about that. As remarkable as God's powerful ingenuity in creating this body that can withstand the minor wounds and illnesses that plague it, my aim is higher than praising God for His perfect design. Oh, I am impressed by this awe-inspiring Maker! He does more than heal our cuts and bruises.

Medical Healing

I continue to expound upon the wonders of our great God. He also provides doctors with the wisdom and skill to bring about healing for complex diseases. This wonderful God of ours has laid out the understanding of His healing processes, has created plants and other medicinal sources on the earth, and has given knowledge to humans on how to use these gifts.

Science and faith are not adversaries. Many feats and marvels of the medical community have saved lives from deadly illnesses by God-given skill. We must humbly realize and remember that without God entrusting His healing knowledge to us, these wonderful gifts would not exist.

Think of the grace and kindness of God. He gave caregivers His unconditional love to use these skills and instincts for our betterment. The wonderful people I have met through my ordeal have nursed and ministered to me through healing and caring. God has given them these instincts and skills that help me. They have a deep desire to use God's gift of healing to keep me healthy despite my paralysis.

The medical community is a gift from God and part of His healing process.

The medical community is a gift from God and part of His healing process. Medical knowledge is not an affront to God's healing power. God uses medical professionals in His toolbox to provide healing for us. He has many avenues and resources to do His work in us. Let us not limit ourselves to one healing method.

Divine Healing

Divine healing refers to when God interrupts nature and heals by His supernatural power. Healing belongs to our God. He can do the impossible (Luke 1:37). Although God ordained healing through natural and medical means, He is the Lord our Healer because He takes more than natural and medical approaches. God intimately connects with us by healing our bodies.

God owes no one an explanation for how He acts. Sometimes He heals with His miraculous power. His reasons may remain unknown to us. Through studying God's Word and how He has revealed himself through His character and deeds, we discover a sovereign God who reserves the right to do whatever He wishes.

We learn more about God the more He interacts with us on an intimate level. Each time God acts, He responds to our situations and shows himself worthy of our praise. He shows us more of His purpose and plan for us and for this world.

When God heals, He teaches us about himself. We discover God's purposes as we study how He heals us. His Word reveals His immense power and divine forethought as He approaches us by His power. Divine healing demonstrates His character concretely to us.

Studying the Bible's Words for Healing

The Hebrew and Greek languages of the Bible have several words for healing. The main two words in Hebrew have similar meaning. The Old Testament overwhelmingly uses the first Hebrew word over sixty times. Its range includes, "heal, restore, remedy, medicine, and physician." Jeremiah uses the second word to describe a covering over a wound as it heals.

In the Greek New Testament, two words are prevalent. We recognize the root of the most prevalent word as a word for therapeutics, meaning to heal or cure. The second word is the medical term for healing or curing disease.

> When God heals, He teaches us about himself.

We see these words when God promises and demonstrates healing. They, along with other words used less often, shape our faith and hope in God to fulfill His promises. We can trust in His ability to heal us. Declare God's promises in your situation, knowing that God maintains His reality over ours.

We use many words for the afflictions we suffer. They range from sickness, illness, disease, disorder, wound, injury, and more. In this book, I use the word "affliction" to refer to these illnesses. When you see the word "affliction," put your malady in place of this word.

It's Not about Me

Though this trial has been hard and continues at the moment of my writing this book, it has taken me to new heights of faith in God and deeper relationships with those around me—especially my parents. God has used this trial to soften my heart, to teach me about empathizing with others, and to harden my resolve and my faith in Him to withstand whatever the devil wishes to throw at me. Now trust me, I'm no showoff. My reason for telling you this is not for you to think what a great person I am. This is not about me. This is about God and the way He teaches us to grow through trials when all we want to do is crumble from the inside out.

Because a trial, as those who have endured one understand, is not about lifting oneself up, but about sharing the incredible grace our Savior gives. A trial can go either way; either it will strengthen and build your faith in God, or it will strengthen and build fear of the future and current circumstances. A trial either makes you or breaks you. You choose which one happens to you.

A trial either makes you or breaks you.

This book is about a subject I have studied in the Bible thoroughly. God has challenged me to believe that when my reality does not match the promise that He has given me, then my reality will change. He challenges me to trust in the future He is writing on my heart and in my body. Healing for me is not some systematic look at a few verses and mentally assenting to what God says in those verses. Healing is an up-close and personal communion between my Lord and me.

I do not write this book to make money or to convince you of some theology. I write to invite you into the ongoing living, breathing discussion between a servant of God and His maker. Healing is not merely some topic of interest to me but an intimate and vibrant growing into the truths and promises of a God who loves me and wants my best. He will fulfill His promises—not always the way I expect or desire, but the way He has planned from the beginning.

> Healing for me is not some systematic look at a few verses and mentally assenting to what God says in those verses.
> Healing is an up-close and personal communion between my Lord and me.

To help and encourage you in your affliction, the end of each chapter has action steps under the heading "Preparing for War" to build your faith to believe God's healing is on its way. I hope these action steps encourage you to wait expectantly and to act on God's promises and principles for healing. We cannot force our healing, but we must not sit around wasting valuable time to minister for the Lord as we wait on His timing.

It's Just Getting Started

I opened my eyes and stared at the ceiling again. I couldn't move. I heard my parents and my younger sister talking. Voices from my church family joined in with them. My first thought as an ordained minister was, *Why are these people in my bedroom? I'm naked! What will they think of me?*

Then I realized this was not my bedroom ceiling. Nurses and doctors assessed my condition and discussed life-flighting me to another hospital with better equipment and specialists. I could barely comprehend my condition. Someone noticed I was awake. They called for the nurses. I was still trying to figure out what was going on.

Several medical professionals surrounded me before I knew what was happening. They asked me if I knew where I was and what had happened to me. They brought my parents and sister over and asked, "Do you know who these people are?"

That's when I realized I had no voice. Thick tubes pushed on the corner of my mouth. How could they understand me with these tubes in the way? Somehow one of them understood. "He knows these are his parents and sister! That's wonderful news!"

Wonderful news? Why wouldn't I recognize my family? "Jonathan, we will ask you yes and no questions. Blink your eyes once for yes and twice for no, so we can all understand you." Finally, someone knew how to communicate.

God is not done with us yet.

"Do you know what happened to you?" I blinked twice.

"Do you know where you are?" I blinked once. I was in some kind of hospital. I imagine it was Reading Hospital. They were close to my house and the only hospital around.

"Do you know these people?" The faces of people from my church appeared, and I blinked once for each of them.

I heard a voice in the background, "He has cognition still. That's great news."

One of the other medical professionals filled me in. "Jonathan, the paramedics and Lucy found you in your room unconscious. We have determined you are paralyzed. The paramedics brought you to Reading Hospital this morning. We don't know the extent of the paralysis."

I was stunned. What caused it? I searched my mind, trying to remember what I would have done to cause paralysis. I couldn't think of anything.

The medical professionals left the room, probably collaborating on how to explain what happened. My family and church friends gathered around me and took turns talking to me. They prayed. I drifted off to sleep again.

The next time I was conscious, I was in a new facility with new voices of doctors assessing my condition. My family was there too. They asked me yes and no questions. I responded with one blink for yes and two blinks for no.

September 25, 2013, changed my life. There were new experiences ahead of me as I would learn to deal with complete paralysis from the neck down. Everything from learning how to operate a wheelchair with the Sip & Puff straw to depending on others for my survival became my new reality. God has taught me a lot in this time, but He is not done with my story yet—and He's not done with you yet, either.

Chapter 1
Acknowledge Your Affliction

> "Therefore, God both exalted and graciously granted to Him
> the name above all names, so that at the name of Jesus,
> every knee shall bow in heaven and on earth and
> under the earth, and every tongue confess that
> Jesus Christ is Lord to the glory of God the
> Father" (Philippians 2:9-11).

Before we can experience God's healing touch, we must acknowledge our affliction. How can God heal us if we are not afflicted? Acknowledging your affliction does not mean accepting it. When we acknowledge our affliction, we make way for God's reality to become ours.

Trusting in God means that He can heal our afflictions even if we don't want to admit we have them. It's not an act of faith to deny what our senses tell us. We must put bad theology to bed. Let us acknowledge our affliction and the One who can change our present reality.

My Job Experience

So, there I was in the hospital bed, unable to move anything but my eyes. The medical professionals feared I would not be able to move my face either, but as the days passed, I gained mobility in my face and neck. Going from blinking my eyes to answering questions, I learned how to answer by people reading my lips despite the tubes at the corner of my mouth.

My mom also learned how to read my lips, which opened a world of communication between a strong mother and her son. The first thing I wanted was for her to read Scripture to me. We started with Psalm 103, and we barely got through it, crying at almost every phrase. As she read it, I was mouthing the words I had memorized. Next, I threw my mom off by asking her to read Job 1-2.

The first two chapters of Job give us the backdrop for his trial. Only the reader reads the spiritual context behind Job's trials. Satan is angry with God because Job is so faithful to Him. But the game is unfair, Satan responds, because God has blessed Job. He says that if God would remove His hedge of blessing from Job, and Job were to endure a bit of suffering, he would turn from God. Satan was sure of it.

> I believed this trial was a challenge
> from the devil to test my faith.

God, foreknowing by Job's character the outcome, allowed Satan to test Job. Unaware of Satan's testing, Job sees his children murdered, his cattle taken away from him, and his health stolen from him. Unaware of Satan, Job believes God is at work. Still, Job does not turn from God. Job believes that God does as He wishes, even if it seems spiteful from a human perspective.

At the end of the first chapter, Job states, "The Lord gives, and the Lord takes away; blessed be the name of the Lord" (Job 1:21). In the second chapter, Job rebukes his wife for telling him to curse God and die (2:9-10). After reading this, my mom asked me if I believed I was about to die. Death was far from my mind. I believed this trial was a challenge from the devil to test my faith, as happened to Job.

Receiving My Diagnosis

When the doctors at Reading Hospital realized their medical equipment was not advanced enough, they gave my parents a choice between a Philadelphia hospital and Hershey Medical Center. My parents chose Hershey because it was closer to their home, and it was a Penn State research hospital. I opened my eyes to different ceiling tiles.

Every morning, a team of neurologists visited my room. The head neurologist examined me first. He took a tongue depressor, broke it in half, poked the soft round part in my arms, legs, and feet. He asked me if I could feel the tongue depressor each time that he poked me. I could feel it.

One test was to distinguish between the sharp and soft parts of the tongue depressor. I could not tell a difference. This told the neurologists that I had feeling, but only at a certain percentage. If I remember correctly, they thought the feeling below my neck was about 75 percent. I could not feel the difference between sharp and soft objects, nor the difference in temperature.

I am one of the most unusual quadriplegics you will ever meet. Most quadriplegics cannot feel. They do not have sensation below their injury. But because I have such an unusual diagnosis, I can feel below mine. This confounds many of my CNAs and nurses. "You're not supposed to feel that" is a common response I get from them.

Neurologists pride themselves on being able to diagnose a condition within three to seven days, but my case took them twenty-one days to diagnose. After around a hundred tests and many questions, they diagnosed me with Acute Transverse Myelitis.

Acute Transverse Myelitis is a general diagnosis for spinal cord injuries. It means that the myelin, a protective sheath around every nerve in the spinal cord, was compromised. They diagnosed it as an acute condition because it happened so quickly and was so severe.

The spinal cord has three sections from top to bottom: cervical, thoracic, and lumbar. My spinal cord was compromised right under my brainstem at C2 and C3. They thought my brainstem had also been compromised. The nerves for your lung muscles start at C4. That's why I'm on a ventilator. The neurologists told me my diaphragm could not help me breathe.

Is This My "New Normal?"

When I woke up at Hershey Medical Center, I had questions for the Lord: "Is this my 'new normal?' Is this all I have now? Will I ever minister behind the pulpit again?" I could not move my body. I answered yes and no questions with my eyes. I could not speak.

I asked the Lord how I would fulfill His call on my life to pastor, preach, and teach. I could do none of those things in this condition. It was one of the darkest times in my affliction. I believe that if I'm breathing and living, God has something for me to do for Him.

What could I do as a quadriplegic without a voice? It was my crisis. I had tied my identity into God's call and the ministry He'd given me. This painful reality put that in question. How do you handle a crisis of faith? How do you not let your current reality make you depressed?

In that moment, I had questions without answers. I cried out to Jesus with prayers from the Psalms: "Why have You forsaken me?" "Where are You?" "Why don't You answer me when I call?" I was living the Job and David life. Had God abandoned me? Was He done with me? The things I loved to do before my paralysis—pastoring, leading, preaching, and teaching—hung in the balance. *What was I* without them? I had tied my identity to what I did instead of who I am. I knew that God can use any affliction or trial to His benefit, but I saw myself as a pastor, preacher, and Bible teacher. I valued the work I did. I didn't see myself as God's special child. All I had was God's call to preach and pastor. I didn't think of myself in any other way.

God was using this trial to give me a wake-up call. All my questions focused on how to serve God. I was still focused on ministry for Christ instead of being in Christ. God did not cause my affliction, but I came to realize that He could use my affliction to teach me how He views me as His child. As I walk through this dark valley, I am learning Jesus is my all.

I was still focused on ministry for Christ instead of being in Christ.

Are you in the questioning phase of your affliction? I've been there. I'm still there sometimes. As you hear more of my story, you will see that God answered my questions—just not in the time I wanted. Patience is hard enough, but it's even harder in the middle of your affliction. Our culture teaches us to look for immediate gratification and instant solutions to problems. We want answers without doing the work. That's not how Jesus grows our faith and character, though. They grow stronger during afflictions and adversity.

Lying on the hospital bed, I was knocking on Jesus's door and looking for answers. I wanted to hear His voice more than ever before. How much of what I did for Him was on *my* terms instead of *His*? How many times had I ignored His voice? I was all ears, but He doesn't always immediately answer all our questions.

Living in this space of seeking God for answers feels so uncomfortable. Dealing with the day-to-day struggles of your affliction grates against all your preconceived notions of who God is, what He does, how He does it, and why you must suffer your affliction. You cannot force Him into a box to get those answers when you want them. Stick with Him. He's not done with you yet.

Speak Your Reality

Some people teach that you should not talk about your affliction because it shows a lack of faith. Why should you pray for healing, asking others to pray for you, and not talk about your healing? By speaking your reality, you are not declaring sickness over yourself but simply stating that you have an affliction and are trusting God for restoration.

If we act as if we are not sick, then we don't need to ask God for healing or have people pray for us. Showing our affliction and suffering proves that we have faith for God to heal us. When we tell others about our affliction, we show our faith and that we are looking to Jesus for healing. If you don't acknowledge your affliction, then for what will you give Jesus praise when He heals you?

> We bring our afflictions to Jesus because He has the power to heal us.

People who came to Jesus for healing acknowledged their affliction. Jesus asked what they wanted Him to do (Matt 20:32; Mark 10:36, 51; Luke 18:41). They were not afraid to talk about their affliction. The crowd could not keep them silent (Matt 9:27; 20:31). The Gospels record that everyone was healed by Jesus (Matt 4:24; 8:16; 12:15; 14:14; Luke 4:40; 6:19). The afflicted did not have to wait long for their healing. Most accounts include the word "immediately." We bring our afflictions to Jesus because He has the power to heal us.

I have heard some Bible teachers teach that speaking your reality accepts your affliction. Speech is powerful, but you do not speak your affliction upon yourself if you acknowledge it before God. No one should be afraid to acknowledge their affliction and be healed. It is false teaching to not acknowledge the truth and reality of what we suffer. As a quadriplegic pastor, I will not consider the claims of such Bible teachers. When people challenge my faith because I am paralyzed, I respond with biblical evidence. They cannot bully me into believing lies. If you think I am too harsh, remember—pastors like me defend the flock as part of their calling.

How do you feel about your affliction? Take it to the Lord. He can handle your hurt, your volatile emotions, and any negative reactions to your affliction. Do not be afraid to be genuine before the Lord. Pour out your heart to God. Let Him heal your emotions, your view of yourself and Him, and heal your brokenness.

Your Affliction Has a Name

How do you feel about your diagnosis? My neurologists and other doctors have told me that they cannot do anything more for me to manage my pain. Science says I will be paralyzed for life, stuck to a bed and a wheelchair. When my neurologists told me that, I responded, "I don"t put my faith in science. My faith is in Jesus."

Some people receive what doctors and neurologists say about their diagnosis as gospel truth, but there is something special about afflictions—they have a name. Many people hear crippling words like *cancer*, *multiple sclerosis*, *ALS*, *brittle bone disease*, *paralysis*, and *terminal* and feel crushed.

However, it is a *good* thing that doctors can name your affliction because the moment your affliction has a name, it must bow to the Lord Jesus Christ. Jesus has the name that triumphs over every other name. No name is greater than His name. So, when you hear the diagnosis for your affliction, lay it at His feet, and praise the Lord Jesus. Your affliction is a conquered foe!

Stand against False Teaching on Healing

God calls ministers like me to shepherd His flock. Shepherds feed, heal, and protect the sheep. One of my duties as a pastor is to protect believers from false teaching. We need to know what we believe, especially about healing, when we face affliction. Throughout the rest of this chapter, I want to call out and dismantle common false teachings on healing. This will prepare you to defend yourself against false teachers.

When I was a young teenager, I was at a Bible Quiz camp when a minister heard about me being legally blind. He asked me if he could pray for me. I never turn down prayer. After he prayed for me, he asked me if I was healed. I was honest with him and told him, "Not yet." He then rebuked me for not receiving my healing!

Ministers who rebuke you because you are not healed when they pray are false teachers. They discourage people from coming to them to pray because they attack the faith of the ones for whom they pray. Anyone who asks you to pray for them for healing has faith. Otherwise, they would not respond altar calls for healing or ask you to pray for them.

> Your faith should never come under fire if you are not healed when people pray for you.

Stepping toward the altar, lifting holy hands to the Lord during prayer, and asking for prayer are proof of great faith. Ministers must praise God for such faith. If a minister criticizes or belittles your faith, ask if that minister had faith while praying for you. Your faith should never come under fire if you are not healed when people pray for you. Your faith is not the only faith that must be questioned.

Take, for instance, the four friends who brought the paralytic man to Jesus (Mark 2:1-12). The Bible says nothing about the faith of the paralytic. Instead, the four friends show so much faith that when they can't reach Jesus because of the crowd, they cause property damage to a house, pulling tiles off a roof to put their paralyzed friend at Jesus's feet. If a minister attacks your faith, point out this account.

Jesus speaks to the paralytic man and heals him. Pay close attention to what the Bible says. "So when Jesus saw *their faith*, He said to the paralytic, 'Son, your sins are forgiven'" (Mark 2:5, emphasis mine). Jesus healed the paralytic based on the faith of his four friends. The person, or persons, who pray for you are just as responsible for faith as you are.

The Word of Faith Movement

The Word of Faith movement believes so strongly in the words we speak having godlike effect that they believe we are gods—that our words have a god's power to take effect. They don't believe Christians get sick, poor, or suffer. However, none of this agrees with Scripture. The writers of the epistles talk about Christians having suffering and trials, and the Gospels point out how difficult it is for the rich to enter the kingdom of God (Mark 10:25; Luke 18:25).

Word of Faith teachers teach that if you suffer or are poor, you then have affliction because you do not believe. They teach that Christians should not be poor, persecuted, or sick. This too is false teaching. The New Testament is replete with teachings on the suffering and persecution of Christians in this evil world.

Jesus teaches that Christians will suffer persecution (Matt 5:10-12, 44). The entire book of James teaches on various kinds of trials (Jas 1:2-4). The New Testament teaches that Christians will endure suffering for Jesus's name (Acts 5:41; 9:16; 15:36) and for righteousness's sake (1 Pet 3:14). Christians will suffer in general (Eph 3:11). We will experience tribulations (Matt 13:21; 24:9; John 16:33; Acts 14:22; Rom 8:35). Since we live in this fallen world, we will experience its effects.

The Bible Trumps Our Experience

Let's consider other false teachings about healing. Some people object to divine healing because they have never experienced it in their lives. What the Bible says, however, trumps our experience. Just because we have never seen healing and miracles in our lives does not mean God won't heal us. Always put what the Bible says above your experience. Don't let that stop you from seeking and receiving your healing.

Here's another one. "Maybe spiritual healing comes first. Isn't God more concerned about the soul than the body?" they say. The Bible says there is no sickness in heaven, however; if God gives us immortal bodies at the Resurrection, why wouldn't He be concerned about our bodies now? The fact that we will have perfect bodies in heaven does not mean that Jesus doesn't heal today, though. God cares about us now and in the future. That's why Jesus died to give us an inheritance.

The Bible does not speak against healing. It promotes healing and restoration. Jesus can—and will—restore us from afflictions now. He shows His power and glory in healing us. Unbelievers cannot refute this powerful testimony. Allow this biblical truth about healing to comfort you in your grief, pain, and suffering.

My first step toward healing was a much healthier tracheostomy and G-Tube surgery. My doctors informed us that I could not keep the NG Tube for feeding and medicine, and the Endotracheal Tube for breathing going through my mouth and down my throat forever. A tracheostomy through my neck and G-Tube in my belly going directly to my stomach would be safer and healthier.

Trach and G-Tube Surgery

At Hershey, they explained it was unhealthy to keep both an orogastric feeding tube and a breathing tube down my throat long term. A tracheostomy is a surgery where they cut a hole in your throat and install a trach, a tube that connects to your trachea so the ventilator can provide oxygen directly to your lungs. The trach, a plastic tube must be changed every month to prevent infection.

So they performed my tracheostomy and installed a G-tube in my belly to feed me and put my meds directly into my stomach. Although I agreed to both surgeries, I'm not sure today that I would have agreed to put a G-tube in. I think they were concerned that I would have a hard time swallowing with a trach.

We were new to this whole situation, so we relied on the professional opinions of the doctors and nurses who had more knowledge and experience with my situation. They told us they could perform the tracheostomy and G-tube surgeries together, and they could do it bedside. I learned later that tracheostomies should be performed in an operating room so that the trach would be put in the center of the neck. Because they did it bedside, only to be performed as an emergency procedure, my trach is slightly off center to the right. This makes it harder to change every month.

We are unsure which doctor performed the surgeries. A tracheostomy is supposed to be done by an ENT. I cannot be certain that this is the type of doctor who performed my tracheostomy. Several mistakes were made that would probably not have been made if I had been an ENT. When I came home, we consulted with an ENT who was angry with what he found when he performed a surgery to try to correct some of the problems with my trach.

Needless to say, some of the anxiety I have toward trach changes stem from the mechanical issues with my tracheostomy and my first trach change. They also decided to do a spinal tap while I was under to gain more of an understanding of my injury. God protected me and brought me through my surgery.

A Big Scare

With a fresh tracheostomy finished, my first trach was put in so that my skin could heal around it, and I was resting comfortably in my bed. As a research hospital affiliated with Penn State University, Hershey Medical Center had nursing students who gained much of their training and experience on real life guinea pigs like me.

I wanted to help the nursing students. So, when they asked me if they could perform trach care, I didn't know what all that entailed but did not mind. This was another big mistake.

Trach care keeps the stoma, the opening of skin around the trach, from becoming infected by regularly cleaning what medical professionals consider to be an open wound. A piece of gauze cut down the middle fits snugly around the plastic trach. Each trach hole should be slightly bigger than the trach itself.

This means that there is a slight bit of air around the trach. Along with this leak, mucus or breaths can leak out as well. The gauze called a drainage sponge, further protects the skin from any toxins that might compromise it.

First, the nurse takes the drainage sponge out. Then with Q-tip soaked in a part-water-part-peroxide mixture, the nurse cleans around the trach. Next, the nurse dries the area with Q-tips and gauze. Finally, the nurse replaces the trach, ties a cloth-like collar that wraps around the neck, and secures the trach in place. Finally, the nurse puts a new drainage sponge around the trach and tightens the trach ties.

This is the procedure the nursing students wanted to practice on me. I didn't know any better, so I agreed. The problem is that *each* of them needed to practice. Only one or two would perform this procedure on me, but it should not have been done the day of my surgery.

As I rested that night, having a hard time falling asleep because of being in a hospital anyway, I started to feel weaker and weaker. I made my raspberry noise to grab my mom's attention. She looked worried every time she came to the bed. What I didn't know was that my trach area was bleeding heavily enough that the night nurse was changing my bedsheets every hour!

The ICU doctor refused to come inspect what the nurse was reporting even though she told him how badly I was bleeding. "Everything will be fine," he said, "Besides, I can't call the surgeon in the middle of the night anyway." So, I went through the night in this condition.

I was barely paying attention early the next morning when the surgeon who performed my tracheostomy was yelling at the ICU doctor: "Why didn't you call me in the middle of the night? This is very serious!"

While I was still awake, they used some kind of skin glue to glue the skin around my trach back together. Apparently, the trach care so early after surgery had allowed my skin to begin separating, and that was why I bled so much. I'm surprised that the ICU doctor did not get reported for such ineptitude.

The surgeon told us not to allow the students to perform trach care on me and not to do trach care for a while. My skin had to heal before that procedure could be done again. By God's grace, I made it through the night. I was very tired and weak that day, but I was not going to die.

Healing the Blind and Paralyzed

When reading Scripture, I pay special attention to the accounts of Jesus healing the blind and the paralyzed. I have been legally blind since birth, and paralyzed for nine years now. Reading and studying passages about the blind and paralyzed increases my faith that Jesus can heal me of everything I have faced.

Jesus heals a paralyzed man in the Gospels (Matt 9:2-8; Mark 2:3-12). This brings me hope and faith that He can heal me. I know that these people are not quadriplegics, but if Jesus can heal a paralytic man, He can heal me. Nothing is too difficult for Jesus. He can do the impossible. It's time to think big, God-sized healing that testifies to God's goodness and power.

We see certain things as impossible, but nothing is impossible for Jesus (Luke 1:37). The Bible does not speak about the paralytic's faith. Jesus sees the faith of his four friends (Mark 2:5). They trust in Jesus's healing power so much that they bring the man and put him in front of Jesus's feet after tearing off the roof.

> It's time to think big, God-sized healing that testifies to God's goodness and power.

When Jesus visits His hometown, the people don't believe in Him (Matt 13:58). Thus, the Bible says, He only did a few miracles there. Jesus uses two things for our healing—our faith and His divine power. Our faith has the power to work Jesus's healing power in us. His resurrection power dwells in us (Rom 8:11). Do you have the faith to see your healing?

I was born with cataracts in both eyes. Even the surgeries I had to try to repair them did not hinder me from believing that Jesus can heal my eyes and give me 20/20 vision. Jesus can do anything.

I feel encouraged when I read in the New Testament about the healing of the blind (Matt 9:27-28; 11:1; 12:22-24; 13:30-31, 53-58; 15:30-31; 20:30-34; 21:23-27; Mark 6:1-6; 7:31-37; 8:22-26; 10:46-53; 11:27-33; Luke 4:18-30; 7:21-22; 14:21; 18:35-45; John 5:3, 9; 10:21; 11:37; Acts 8:4-8). I have believed from a young age that Jesus can heal my blindness. I believe He will heal me of my blindness the same time He heals me of paralysis.

I know Jesus can heal me of paralysis because He healed paralytics in the Gospels and in Acts through the ministry of the apostles (Matt 4:24; 8:6; 9:2-6; Mark 2:1-10; Luke 5:18-24; John 5:3; Acts 8:7; 9:33). We look to the Bible for faith and find the God who heals our afflictions.

God's Power, Protection, and Peace

God protects us from harm, but we don't need to test Him by putting ourselves in dangerous positions. When I unknowingly agreed to the procedures of my surgery, though, God protected me from the danger of death and watched over me.

You can trust that Jesus watches over you and protects you from harm. Nothing surprises Him. Even if you don't know the possible harm you are in, Jesus knows. He foresees everything that could happen to us. When we are surprised by our situation, we cry out to Him. He already knows, and He puts us at ease. Every time I have a trach change, I ask Jesus for His peace, and He gives it to me.

God has great power, and He uses it as He wills. Even if something bad happens to us, He foresaw it. He surrounds us with His protection. We can walk in peace knowing He is with us. He goes before us. Trust in God's protection and peace. Let it calm you in the midst of your storm.

Our Great and Mysterious God

People want answers for everything. They want a calculated faith, that there's no mystery to God. Tell that to Job, who heard from God but still was not told why he suffered. God does not always answer our questions, and even when He does, it seems to just provoke more questions.

We cannot completely figure God out. His ways are higher than ours (Isa 55:9). God does not operate within our limited capacity to understand Him. Nor does He need our permission to heal us whenever or however He does. I've been paralyzed for nine years, and never once have I told God that my healing is taking too long—because I remain in awe of the Lord and know that fearing Him is the beginning of wisdom, as Scripture says (Prov 9:10). Christians today need to cultivate that fear and awe of the Lord.

I enter God's presence with a healthy fear of who He is and what my place is before Him. The fear of the Lord has two definitions; it speaks of His power and majesty, and it relates to how we revere Him because of His power.

When did we get the idea that we should not be afraid of God? Yes, we are His children, not children of His wrath (Eph 2:3), but He does discipline us. As C. S. Lewis says through the mouth of the male beaver about Aslan in *The Lion, the Witch, and the Wardrobe*, "Safe? ... safe? 'Course he isn't safe. But he's good."[1]

We should maintain a healthy fear of God's power. If we were still sinners, God's judgment would rain down on us in pelts of fiery drops. Let's not get so comfortable with Him because we are not objects of His wrath. We must continue to revere Him for His goodness and greatness, but let's thank God we are not on His "bad side."

> **I choose to believe that to encourage others, Jesus can use my faith in Him despite my paralysis.**

God is the sovereign King of the universe. We don't know half of what He's capable of. I don't try to heal myself. I do not feel angry with God because my time for complete healing has not arrived yet. Despite my circumstances, Jesus remains worthy of my praise. He does not ask for it. I give it freely.

And when these bones are under my power to move, and He makes my muscles strong enough to bear my weight and move me at my command, I assure you, He will never hear the end of the praises I will lift toward heaven! People will never stop hearing me give my testimony! Nonetheless, I praise Him now as I am able.

God is cloaked in mystery. When His presence came down on Mount Sinai, a thick blackness and smoke swirled around Him. Though, as the Apostle John says, "God is light," (1 John 1:5),

---

[1] C. S. Lewis, *The Chronicles of Narnia* (New York: HarperCollins Publishers, 1956), 146.

mystery surrounds Him for now. God chose not to reveal the mystery of the gospel until the New Testament. Though He dwells in some mystery now, He still can search our hearts and know us (Ps 139:23).

I feel encouraged by God's mysteries. He can do things I cannot comprehend or imagine. That fact continues to give me hope. Doctors cannot figure out my condition. Neurologists marvel that I can feel, even if not 100 percent. Science has no solutions for me, but God will heal me and confound the wisdom of this world. I know a Man who holds the power of creation in His hand, and His pinky finger does more than creation can hope for. My hope is in Him alone.

My faith in Jesus does not require me to have all the answers but to trust that Jesus is greater than anything I face and has ultimate power. He does not have to explain everything to me. Sickness does not negate His power. I choose to believe that to encourage others, Jesus can use my faith in Him despite my paralysis.

We don't need all the answers. We trust that Jesus knows what He's doing. In His time, He will do *what* He wants to do—and *how* He wants to do it. He will fulfill His promises *when* He desires. I'm fine with the mystery and the wonder of His plan and process. He has infinite perspective and judgment. I am merely the clay He molds into whatever He wishes me to be.

Take Your Trials with Grace

James tells us to consider trials joy (Jas 1:2), but I have a hard time feeling joy during trials. He explains why in the following verses (vv. 3-4)—because God uses trials to build up our character. He doesn't always cause the trials, but He uses them for His purposes.

God does not give us afflictions, but He uses them to work on us. He uses adversity to make us stronger in Him. At Hershey, one of the nurses introduced me to my first air mattress. It aggressively pushed my body side to side, mimicking turning my body to save the nurse's time. My face stuck in the crevices of the mattress, and I freaked out. My mind told me I would suffocate, even though I don't breathe through my nose anymore. They had to medicate me to calm me down.

I could have handled my experience with my new mattress better. In the midst of a trial, we struggle to find joy. We can't see the end from the beginning as God sees it. Perhaps if we could face trials head on and think about how God is using the trial to make us more like Jesus, we might have more joy in them.

Our afflictions give us the opportunity to grow. That's not their original purpose, but we must try to see how our afflictions give us room to grow. I sometimes lose my temper at my paralysis. It doesn't happen often, but when it does, I feel so bad about how I lash out at people who take care of me.

I imagine how I would react to someone if I were taking care of them, and they lashed out in anger against me. I realize it's not their fault. It's no one's fault. God has shown me that I desire to control the situation, but that is the very thing I cannot do. Daily, I learn more about my mirage idea that I control anything—and about God's sovereignty to control all things.

When I lash out in anger over my paralysis, that keeps me from the notion of control. God reminds me that I control nothing except the opportunity to turn it over to Him. God does not cause our afflictions, but He teaches us amid them. We must be attentive to what we can learn in our adversity.

Is It Physical or Spiritual?

Our afflictions present both physical and spiritual barriers in our lives. We cannot solve them by medical science alone. Each of us is in a spiritual battle. The devil wants to afflict you. You must stand and declare Jesus's victory over your body and against the enemy.

That's why I include action steps entitled, "Prepare for War" at the end of each chapter in this book We cannot sit idly by and allow the enemy any ground. Don't look only for physical solutions to your affliction. Realize that the enemy wants you afflicted. He doesn't want you to stand with God's power behind you and fight him.

Satan tried to kill me. He tried to shut me up because of what I was preaching and teaching. I underestimated my power in the spiritual realms—but no more. I want that same victory and fight for you. Let us stand as Paul commanded (Eph 6:10-14) and take the fight to the enemy. We are seated with Christ in heavenly places (2:6). Don't let the devil steal your voice!

Prepare for War

- What is your affliction? Acknowledge it. Don't let it control you.
- As you acknowledge your affliction before Jesus, ask Him to heal you from it. Your freedom is spiritual and physical.
- How can you take your stand against the enemy? Every time I preach, I declare that I'm kicking the enemy in the teeth. What is your "take it to the enemy" strategy? Write an action plan of resistance.

Chapter 2
Believe God's Promises

"He said, 'If you will surely heed the voice of the Lord your God and do what is right in His eyes, and listen to His commandments, and keep all His statutes, then I will put none of the diseases on you that I put on the Egyptians, for I am the Lord your Healer'" (Exodus 15:26).

At Hershey Medical Center, I endured the beginning days of my paralysis. Kind and well-meaning doctors and neurologists tended to me, tried to explain my injury, and were the stopgap that saved my life. It was a place of struggle, of understanding what happened to me, and a place where I refused to give up or give in.

In my darkest moments, I remembered what I have learned all my years of studying God's Word. Those things sustained and encouraged me, building me up when life tore me down. Jesus is my anchor, so I trusted in God's promises for healing. The doctors saw an impossible paralysis, but I trust in the God of the impossible. In this chapter I will share with you God's healing promises that strengthen my faith every day and give me hope for my healing.

Connecting with My Mom

I've told you about my mom reading Scripture to me when I first arrived at Hershey Medical Center. My faith had not wavered because of this paralysis. I knew that Satan had done this to me, trying to shut me up. Even though he took my voice for a moment, he could not take my mind or my life. My life belongs to Jesus, and only He can take it away. Instead, God has given me eternal life, and even if I would have died in my bed at home or in a hospital bed, I would live again with Him.

When I asked my mom to read my favorite Psalm (103), we barely got through it, crying at almost every phrase. As she read it, I was mouthing the words I had memorized in the past. The Psalm commands the soul to bless the Lord. The Bible doesn't mention the circumstances under which David wrote this Psalm.

> My mom and I cried through every phrase of that Psalm.

I understand this passage to say that no matter how dark our circumstances, we have no excuse to not bless the Lord. He deserves our praise even if we walk through the valley of the shadow of death. The benefits of the Lord outweigh the heaviness of suffering our afflictions.

David lists at least five benefits of knowing the Lord. He forgives us, heals us, redeems us, crowns us with love and mercy, satisfies us with good, and renews us (Ps 103:1-5). The Lord is so good to us. My mom and I cried through every phrase of that Psalm. Remember—your affliction does not change anything Jesus has promised to do in you.

Jesus has promised healing, and I hold onto that promise every day. His promises remain an anchor for the soul. They go deep into the heart of my identity. The day-to-day sufferings and setbacks I face are on the surface of the water while His promises hold my feet on the rock under them. They may buffet me, but my faith in Jesus's promises grounds me in Him.

My mom and I had the understanding that this paralysis was momentary and that Jesus had my back. This wasn't the end of my story. When I prayed that day, "Whether I live or die, it's for God's glory, and because I am alive, I know you are not finished ministering through me," I knew God's call on my life was still my main objective. The devil had tried to shut me up, but his failure is my game.

God's Promises for Healing

The Bible has many promises of physical healing and examples of people being healed of physical affliction. One of God's names, *Yahweh Rapheka (Jehovah Raphah)* means, "I am the Lord, Your Healer." The Israelites had just left Egypt, and in their travels in the wilderness, they could not find water.

They ended up at Marah, which means, "bitter water" (Exod 15:22-26) The people became angry with Moses, and Moses asked the Lord for help. God showed Moses a log, and when he threw it into the water, the water became sweet. God identified himself by saying, "I am the Lord your Healer" (Exod 15:26).

We can apply this promise in God's name to our situation because God does not change (Mal 3:6; Heb 13:5; Jas 1:17). No one is certain if this name for God is connected to the blessings and curses of the covenant in Deuteronomy 28 or if it refers to God not putting on Israel the diseases He put on Egypt. Either way, as part of God's name, "The Lord your Healer," God is the great Physician who protected the Israelites from diseases.

If God's name connected to the blessings of people in Deuteronomy 28, then violating the covenant would make a person susceptible to those diseases. There is an element of obedience to this promise from God found in His name. God's names in the Bible come from experiences people have with Him. Because God protected the Israelites from the bitter water, He proclaimed himself their healer.

God's name applies to us today. He is our Healer who protects us from illness and gives us His power as our great physician. He created the body, and He can heal anything, even quadriplegic paralysis. Nothing is too difficult for Him. The people grumbled against God and Moses because of the bitter waters they could not drink, but Moses prayed to God, and God gave him the solution to the bitter water. God directed Moses to the right log to throw into the water to change it.

When we pray and ask God for healing, He readily answers us. We may not like the answer, especially if it is, "Not yet," but God answers our prayers and heals our infirmities. We can rely on Him when modern medicine and science fail us.

> "Heal me, and I will be healed" (Jer 17:14).

Later in Israel's history, King Hezekiah had a terminal illness (2 Kgs 20:5). When the prophet informed the king he would die, Hezekiah turned toward the wall and prayed a fervent, desperate prayer to the Lord with tears. God answered his prayer and granted him fifteen more years.

God can reverse any affliction in our bodies. So, if we don't question His power to heal, maybe like the leper in Luke 17:11-, we may wonder if God wants to heal us. The leper said to Jesus, "Lord, if you will, you can make me clean." Jesus did not leave any room for doubt when He answered, "I will. Be clean." Jesus wants to heal you.

Maybe you think you don't deserve to be healed, or that God is too busy to heal you. The Gospels tell us that Jesus has healing for all (Matt 9:35; Luke 6:19). Part of Jesus's suffering and death on the Cross guarantees our healing (Isa 53:4-5; 1 Pet 2:24).

We can trust that the Lord has both the power and the will to heal us. Jeremiah says the promise well: "Heal me, and I will be healed" (Jer 17:14). God will take away sickness and heal you (Exod 23:25; Deut 32:29; Jer 33:6). Cry out to the Lord concerning your infirmity; He will send His word and heal your disease (Ps 30:2; 107:20-21).

God further reveals His promises throughout Scripture. He promises healing for the blind and those bowed down (Ps 146:8). He restores the sick to health (Jer 30:17). God heals your disease (Ps 103:2-3).

God desires for you to live in health. His love keeps you from death (Isa 38:17). God's statutes bring life (Prov 4:20-23). The sun will rise with healing in its wings (Mal 4:2). Jesus took your infirmity (Matt 8:17). The prayer of faith will heal the sick (Jas 5:14-16).

All of these promises and examples of healing increase our faith. I turn to the Bible for encouragement, comfort, and to remember God's promises of healing. These promises were not only for Bible times. They are for you and me. In trying times of our afflictions, we can run to God's Word and hear from Him.

The God of Life and Death

Genesis gives us insight into God's ability to both give life and take it away. Many attribute sickness to sin, for which they are partially correct in their portrayal of the origins of sickness. It is not the whole story. Because God is sovereign, all things fall under His providence, including sickness.

God controls the beginning of life and its end. He gives knowledge and wisdom to human beings teaching them how to do what He does. We see people who learn the principles of healing from God and show them as healers in their communities, but the origins of these powers come from God.

God creates life and has the power to heal. He alone holds knowledge and sovereignty over creation. He controls the beginning and end of life. We must not be afraid of death, because He decides the number of our years upon this earth.

The creation song of Genesis 1 teaches us that God did not create by mistake or by accident, as the creation myths of the time of Moses did. God creates with purpose and meaning. Things do not happen by chance or by accident. No matter how silent God may seem in our afflictions, He walks beside us every step of the way.

God continues to create with purpose as Genesis 2 shows us by zooming in on God's creation of humanity and how He acted with divine order and purpose. God set up creation as the perfect model intended for humanity.

Sickness and death were not part of God's creation; He foresaw them and can use them to strengthen us and increase our faith. However, He had only good things for us in the beginning, and still does today. Humanity brought sin and its consequences into the world but had help in the accuser and adversary, Satan.

Hope and faith are the keys to living between God's healing promises and their fulfillment.

Adam and Eve's choice opened them up to a fallen world. Their rebellion and sin gave sickness and death the opportunity to infect humanity. Sin is not the only cause of sickness, but both can lead to death. Healing is part of salvation, available to everyone who trusts in Jesus, who heals us completely—soul, body, and mind. Hope and faith are the keys to living between God's healing promises and their fulfillment. God's plan for you is not yet complete. We suffer the effects of this fallen creation, but Jesus provides healing to us.

The account of the beginning of sin, sickness, and death lays the foundation for understanding healing in the Old Testament. Because of the connection of sin with death, a common belief of sin causing sickness emerged. However, faith conquers that old story and brings Jesus's healing to our bodies and souls.

Turn to the Source of Healing

People turn to many sources of healing—shamans, medicine men, witch doctors, physicians, and medicines. There is no shortage of spiritual leaders who claim to heal diseases of all kinds. But none of them can do what Jesus can do. In the Bible, sick people also looked to other spiritual sources than God. But when Jesus came, He healed people as He proclaimed the arrival of the kingdom of God—and He still heals today.

Jesus is our source of healing. When He shows up, powerful miracles happen. Several of the accounts of healing in John are close to my heart and build my faith. The invalid in John 5 did not know who Jesus was. Instead, he relied on a myth for his healing. He soon found out, though, what Jesus does.

How many times do we look to other sources for healing instead of Jesus? John 5:4 (not in many translations of the Bible due to textual issues), explains the responses of the invalid who put his faith in a pool of water for healing. This account is quite telling because Jesus asks penetrating, perceptive questions. Imagine you had been paralyzed for thirty-eight years. You didn't know about Jesus and His healing power. All you knew was a myth about an angel stirring the waters of a certain pool. All you had to do was get in the pool first. But that was an impossible goal since you are paralyzed.

You have placed all your hopes in getting into the pool first after a mythical angel stirs it. Someone had to stir the waters—but not just anyone. The reason the pool was special is because of the one who stirs it.

Without John 5:4, the passage doesn't make any sense. When it says an angel stirs the pool and the first person in is healed, it makes supernatural sense. As they do today, people then believed in angels because they were God's messengers with special powers. Without this piece of information, we won't know who stirs the pool.

It seems this man believed in this myth; he placed his faith in it for his healing. His faith was in an impossible goal as a paralytic to be the first in the pool after an angel would stir it. He may sound crazy, but people place their faith in many improbable promises.

What are you investing your time and energy into for your healing?

This man invested his time and energy into trying to get into the pool (John 5:6). What are you investing your time and energy into for your healing? There's only one source for divine healing: Jesus Christ.

Jesus asks a powerfully perceptive question of the man: "Do you want to be healed?" (John 5:6). The longer you have an illness or disability, the more you get used to it. You begin thinking this is a normal lifestyle. You stop praying. Little by little, you stop believing you need healing. You let time and circumstance change your persistence in seeking Jesus for healing.

Are you in such a place? Have you settled for less than God's best? In the Gospels, people waited for healing from twelve to thirty-eight years. Then Jesus healed them in an instant. Blind people refused to allow the crowds to sway them from shouting for Jesus to heal them. Have you lost your desire for His healing touch? Renew your desire for Jesus's healing. Seek Him with the same persistence of the woman seeking justice from an unjust judge (Luke 18:1-8).

> ## Have you lost your desire for His healing touch?

This man was persistent in his own way, but he had set his faith on an impossible source for healing. After many years of paralysis and waiting on the impossible healing for a stirred pool he could not get into first, you would think the man would question this method of healing.

But he was still there. He had real faith, but it was misplaced. He believed in the wrong source of healing. When Jesus asked His question, the man does not answer yes or no. His focus was no longer on healing. He provided an excuse for why he wasn't healed yet.

Do you have excuses for not pursuing divine healing? "Sir, I don't have a person to put me in the pool when the water is stirred" (John 5:7). This man realized he couldn't do it by himself. We all know our limitations.

I must have someone caring for me 24/7. Every two hours, I need a drink. I take medicine throughout the day. If my tubes disconnect from my vent, I can only breathe on my own for so long before I need my vent reattached. Every so often, my limbs need moving. I constantly depend on those around me for my survival.

At that pool, someone else would always beat that paralyzed man to the punch. He knew the flaws in the object of his faith. With just one command from the Savior in the matter of seconds, the man could be completely healed. If only he knew the Source of healing. But at the point of his interaction with Jesus, he still doesn't know that it's Him.

The man wasn't the only person waiting to get into this pool. There were other paralyzed people as well as the blind and lame. The man couldn't beat the people in front of him to get into the pool first. There are many such popular approaches to healing that don't yield results. Only Jesus can heal someone who needs divine physical healing. We must put our faith in Jesus and in His guidance on our treatment and other sources of healing.

In Acts 3, a lame beggar sits at the entrance to the Jerusalem temple looking for alms. He is relying on the charity of anyone who passes by and would show him pity. He's milking the system for all it's worth. He directs his attention to those who seem like they'll give him a handout. That is the only reason he directs his gaze toward Peter and John. When Peter tells him to look at him, the man thinks Peter has money to give to him. Imagine his dismay when Peter says, "Silver and gold don't belong to me." It must have been a big letdown. But Jesus has something greater.

"But what I have, I give to you."

Peter finishes that thought with, "But what I have, I give to you. In the name of Jesus Christ of Nazareth, walk." Such a simple command. The man is shocked and maybe afraid as Peter grabs his right hand and pulls him up. I would feel unsure if someone tried to help me out of my bed without the proper equipment.

The man looks down at his legs and feet. To his surprise, the years of atrophy to his leg, ankle, and feet muscles reverse, and be begins to bulk up. His muscles become strong as Peter pulls him up. He didn't have to go to rehab. His response is fitting. He tests out his healed legs walking around, and then he goes with Peter and John into the temple walking and leaping and praising God. The man had watched everyone around him for years because he could not move, but now he gives God the glory and praises Him for his healing.

Nights in Hershey Medical Center

My condition made it impossible to sleep in the hospital. I don't sleep well in unfamiliar places but being paralyzed kept me up at night. The night nursing staff probably thought I was a holy terror. I didn't have a call bell to get their attention. I started using the sound of my lips pressed together with a slight push of breath through them.

Thus, I 'blew raspberries' when I needed their help. Because I could not sleep or adjust to my new surroundings, I got their attention throughout the night. I was alone with my thoughts. My mind took me between desperation, inquiring of the Lord why this had happened to me, wondering what the future held, and mourning the loss of my abilities.

But more than my thoughts of my changed situation were the comforting words I had memorized from the Bible. I repeated them throughout the nights at Hershey Medical Center. Jesus reassured me that this was not the end. My situation had not surprised Him. To be sure, it shocked me, changed my world, and left me with questions about my call to preach the gospel and pastor God's people—but He wasn't surprised.

The devil does his worst in the darkness, but the light of Jesus and His Word sustained me. I repeatedly claimed the truths of Scripture. I did battle with evil thoughts and determined to believe God's promises. Some people call it blind faith, but faith guided me out of fear, anxiety, worry, and loss. I believed the story Jesus was writing and chose joy, trust, and patience. *I didn't win those battles; Jesus's power in me and my relationship with Him got me through them and still does today.*

Bible Prayers and Encouragement for Healing

As we read Scripture, we can pray along with the biblical saints for our healing. Some prayers for healing include Isaiah 38:16, where he says, "Restore me to health." The psalmist cries, "Heal me, O Lord" (Ps 6:2). We can go to God at any time, and He hears our requests. Sometimes I think my requests are so mundane that I should not pray about them, but no matter our request, it does not bore God.

I sometimes pray through my to-do list. It helps clear my mind so I can concentrate on talking to God every day. Our afflictions may keep us up at night, but God's door is still open. Prayer is the fastest way to talk to God. We can pray about our affliction, and He hears our prayers and responds to us. He knows the pain, suffering, crying, and pleading we do with Him.

> When your affliction makes you feel weak or sick, cry out to Jesus.

Isaiah encourages us that God gives strength to the weak and faint (Isa 40:29). Just a chapter later, God promises He is with us and will strengthen and uphold us (41:10). Proverbs instructs us to have a joyful heart instead of a crushed spirit (Prov 17:22). Medical professionals attest to the positive attitude of a patient and its constructive effect on health.

When your affliction makes you feel weak or sick, cry out to Jesus. Jesus gives us the strength to face each day. He walks with us, strengthens us, and gives us peace. How do you feel after you cry out to God? Because He's always with us, we feel His quiet peace, like the friend we can always call. He makes our painful experiences bearable.

The Psalms are full of encouragement. God's promise gives us life (Ps 119:50). Many turn to Psalm 103:3, which says that God heals us. Jeremiah speaks faith into God's promises for healing when he says, "Heal me, and I shall be healed" (Jer 17:14). We need to encourage one another and build up our faith in God's promises. Scripture teaches us that God has never failed at keeping and fulfilling His promises. We fail Him in questioning His promises or in being impatient. Let us pray that we can wait on His timing.

Jesus promises rest for the weary (Matt 11:28). Paul instructs us that when we become anxious with our afflictions to bring our request to God in prayer (Phil 4:6-7). He tells us God began a good work in us and will complete it (Phil. 1:6). Jesus gives us rest just when we need it. Do you take Jesus up on His provision of rest? In our busy schedules and lifestyles, we must take the moments of rest Jesus provides for us and not keep running ourselves ragged.

Commit to Have Timeless Faith

When I get discouraged or need some encouragement, I think about the fact that faith is timeless. We have waited for Jesus to return in His Second Coming in the clouds for over two thousand years now—and yet, He could come back at any time. My faith in His return will not wane even if that return does not happen in my lifetime.

Faith reaches across the ages. It doesn't have an expiration date or time limit. This encourages me because I have been paralyzed since

2013. When I think of the time that I have been in this condition, I get discouraged if I dwell on it.

Yet faith lives for the hope of the promise to be fulfilled. It doesn't matter how long it takes. Faith is beyond time. It reaches into the future and hopes in God's healing. I am determined to never think that time will change the result of God's will for my healing. Jeremiah lived with the same people who cursed him because of his prophecies. I'm sure he was beaten while in prison, but he never gave up on God. He simply said, "Heal me, and I will be healed" (Jer 17:14). That simple statement of faith does not raise a care about how long it takes.

Let your trust expand beyond the borders of time. Don't let time or the enemy steal your joy.

Jesus can heal immediately, and He may have a special time to heal. We ask questions about why Jesus hasn't healed us yet or how long it's going to take Him to do it. We are the ones who allow time to affect our faith. Let's settle once and for all that Jesus *will* heal us. The rest is up to Him. Don't allow time to steal the joy of the hope on which your faith is founded.

Faith stretches beyond the grasp of time, seizing timeless truth and putting hope to work in us. Time only steals our joy if we allow it to. Let your trust expand beyond the borders of time. Don't let time or the enemy steal your joy.

How Does Jesus Heal?

Gospel writers use the word immediately seventy-seven times in the original language. Jesus heals immediately throughout the Gospels; even when He doesn't heal in person, it is at that very hour when people figure out that the healing took place.

In a few places, God heals progressively. Progressive healing works over time. God gave creation ability to heal on its own. Our bodies have extraordinary ability to heal themselves. God gives wisdom and skill to doctors and powerful medicines to heal us. For instance, Elisha instructed Naaman to wash in the Jordan seven times before he was healed (2 Kgs 5:14). Jesus did not heal the ten lepers immediately. They were healed as they went to the priest (Luke 17:14).

One account of progressive healing happens to the blind man who sees men "as trees walking" (Mark 8:23-26). Jesus leads the man out of the city, perhaps to do something special. Then He spits on his eyes and lays His hands on him. The people in the crowd beg Jesus to touch the blind man. Perhaps Jesus led the man away from them because they were miracle chasers, wanting to see Jesus do something just to see it.

Jesus isn't interested in impressing others with how He heals. He heals because He is glorious. He heals out of compassion and love for us. The people were trying to direct Jesus on how to heal. He touches the blind man, but spits on his eyes first. Jesus does things His way. Don't tell Jesus how to heal you. Just glorify His name when He does.

> Jesus does things His way. Don't tell Jesus how to heal you. Just glorify His name when He does.

Jesus did not declare that the man could see. Instead, He asked the man if he could see anything. This is the most common approach I have seen by faith healers and preachers who pray for the sick. They ask if a person can do things with the disabled part of their body that they couldn't do before.

When the man looked, he could see people as trees walking. He saw basic shapes but not details. He laid His hands on the man's eyes again. When the man opened his eyes, he could see clearly. Then Jesus sent the man to his house instead of into the village. Jesus does not heal for some sideshow or spectacle; He heals so we can glorify Him.

We can speculate for ages why Jesus heals this blind man progressively. Does this show that God doesn't always work immediately? Is progressive healing any less glorifying to God? However God heals you, it is always glorious. Don't be concerned with how God heals you. He has given you back full faculty and health. Always give praise to Jesus for your healing—no matter how He does it.

How Is the Holy Spirit Involved in Healing?

Oil is one symbol of the Holy Spirit in Scripture. His anointing power comes through the ceremonial pouring of oil over the commissioned person (e.g., Aaron, kings, priests, prophets). James instructs church elders to anoint the sick and pray over them (Jas 5:14). Anointing with oil symbolizes the Holy Spirit coming upon the sick and working a powerful healing miracle in them. Do you ask your church elders to anoint you with oil and pray for you?

Some of the nine spiritual gifts Paul lists in 1 Corinthians 12:8-10 include the gifts of faith, healings, and miracles. Not all Christians have these gifts, but they must have faith to please God (Heb 11:6). Every Christian must have faith in Jesus, in His saving work on the Cross, and in His power to change our lives and the world. Those with the gift of faith have greater faith to see God do amazing and miraculous things. They trust God so deeply that they ask for huge things and see God do them.

The Holy Spirit can give the gift of healing to evangelists who see miracles of healings in people who remain unconvinced of God's power or who feel desperate for their healing and have faith. Healing often happens in Scripture to show God's power. We should not limit the gift of healing to evangelists. Christians who have the gift of faith may also have the gifts of healing and miracles.

The Holy Spirit distributes these gifts as He wills and sees fit (1 Cor 12:7). Christians with the gifts of faith, healings, and miracles must learn how to follow the Holy Spirit's prompting and hone their gifts. They must believe God for powerful miracles.

No Christian is exempt from praying for the sick or having faith to believe God for miracles. These gifts do not mean you don't have to believe God and have faith or trust Him to heal your affliction. God can use mustard seed-sized faith to do the impossible (Matt 17:20). You must believe that Jesus can heal your disease when you see God's miracles in the Bible. So, have faith in God's power to heal your affliction. A little faith is all God needs to do impossible miracles.

Using Doctors and Medicine

I must take medicine every day for paralysis and nerve pain. I see neurologists and doctors regularly for updates on my condition from a scientific and medical analysis perspective. This brings up an important question. Does going to doctors and using medicine mean that we have given up on God's promise for divine healing? Is it OK to go to doctors?

God gave doctors the medical skill and know-how to help us manage our condition until Jesus heals us. It's not wrong to go to doctors or to use medicine. I personally try to stay away from addictive medicine. If I must use it, I try not to use it so often that

I become addicted. I see addiction as slavery to another master. You must decide how doctors and medicine factor into your condition.

Doctors and medicines can provide relief in our afflictions. It took a while after I came home until I found a neurologist who helped me control my nerve pain. I still have bad days when the weather suddenly changes or we get rain or snow, all of which affects my pain level. Other than these sudden changes, my pain level stays very low. I thank God for doctors and medicines that can help with the side effects of paralysis.

You may have personal reasons for not going to doctors or not using the medicine they prescribe. The Bible does not say that going to doctors is wrong. The woman with the issue of blood went to many doctors. However, they could not help her, just as doctors cannot heal my paralysis. Luke was a doctor, and there are caregivers throughout the Scriptures like the four friends of the paralytic man and the good Samaritan who bound the wounds of the attacked man. God provided medical professionals and caregivers to bless us and help us until Jesus heals us.

Moving on from Hershey

I spent four weeks at Hershey Medical Center where they diagnosed me, put a trach in my neck and G-tube in my belly, and stabilized me. However, I couldn't stay in that hospital forever. It was time to move on to the next step God had for me. I headed to Philadelphia to MaGee Rehab Hospital. I wondered how much rehabilitation they could do for me.

Instead of living in the past, move to your future. See what God is bringing to you now and what lies ahead.

I would soon find out. I left behind the place of my injury and the place of some of my greatest struggles. It was a new day with new mercies from God. The next step in my adventure awaited me. I would spend eight weeks at MaGee. I learned how to navigate my quadriplegia. Some things would feel encouraging, and some things would feel discouraging. None of that would change my resolve, though; the next chapter in my life had begun.

We often focus on our past wounds and hurts, dwelling on the beginning of our affliction, why God hasn't healed us, and question God. Instead of living in the past, move to your future. See what God is bringing to you now and what lies ahead. God has good things for you. His healing isn't in the past. Walk with God in faith. Only He can see you through the hard times.

Preparing for War

Which of the Bible promises and examples sticks out to you? Pray these promises to God. Live as though your healing has happened.

I have created a playlist on Spotify and Amazon Music called the "Rough Road for My Miracle." You can play those songs that encourage your faith in God's healing promises.

Chapter 3
Pray for Your Healing

> "Is anyone sick among you? He must summon the elders of the
> assembly and they must pray for him and anoint him with oil
> in the name of the Lord. And the prayer of faith will deliver
> the sick and the Lord will raise him up. And if he has
> committed sins, he will be forgiven. Therefore,
> confess to one another sins and pray for one
> another, that you might be healed.
> Very powerful is the entreaty of
> the righteous person while it
> is working" (James 5:14-16).

As you continue to walk the path of complete healing for your affliction, you have acknowledged your affliction and believe in God's promises for healing. Next, you need to put your faith into action by praying for your healing.

God uses trials like little steppingstones to increase our faith. Each trial brings the need for more faith in God to do His work in your life. But what do you do with setbacks? Does it affect your faith? How do you keep your faith in God's promises and in His track record when your reality says you're moving backward?

Prayer is your lifeline to Jesus during your affliction. It increases your faith, guides your way, gives you comfort and peace. In this chapter, I talk about how faith ministers to me in my paralysis. God is just a prayer away. He's always available to hear us.

Going to Rehab at MaGee

Paramedics and an ambulance transported me from Hershey Medical Center in Hershey, PA at the end of October 2013 to MaGee Rehabilitation Hospital in Philadelphia. Being at rehab was another new experience for me. Their goal was to help me understand my limitations and to give me independence.

I was excited to be moving on from Hershey Medical Center. The doctors and nurses there were very good to me but limited in scope. They could not tell me how to deal with my paralysis or to navigate my change in lifestyle.

Medical professionals greeted me when I arrived at MaGee. They gave me boots for my feet that kept them off the bed. My heels thanked them. I experienced a lift for the first time. First, they put a lift pad under you with straps on it. They hook the straps to the lift machine, and it picks you up off the bed. This is how I get from my bed to my chair. They had a fancy one that came down from the ceiling. I sensed immediately that things would be different for me there than at the hospital.

I looked around my new room—so different from my hospital room. It was a large room with tan walls. There was a place with a giant mirror and sink to prepare for each day. To my right was a giant wall-to-wall window to look out on the city. I didn't have roommates.

An aid showed me how to operate my call bell. It was a long, slender plastic tube that the aid could manipulate in every direction. At the end was a straw that I could blow through to activate the call bell light outside my room.

I had a unique bed. It had an air mattress, unlike the one at the hospital. The therapist turned it on, and as it started turning, I asked her to turn it back off. I have an aversion to the aggressive turning. I shared my experience with air mattresses at Hershey with the therapist, and she turned it to a lower level. Moving mattresses keep your skin from getting bedsores.

One of my favorite functions of the air mattress was the ability to gently shake me, a therapeutic technique for loosening the mucus in my lungs for suctioning. It just felt good. After being stuck in an uncomfortable hospital bed for a month, this was a very acceptable change.

A Crisis of Fear

I had just arrived at MaGee Rehabilitation Hospital and was getting comfortable in my new surroundings. There were some promising things happening in my life. Just being out of the hospital was a step forward. The prospect of rehab made me hopeful for my future, that this paralysis would not last forever.

The first full day at MaGee, they wanted me to get out of bed and start a routine. They made a wheelchair that fit me perfectly. The day I came, a wound care group came and scoured my body for any open areas or skin problems from the hospital.

But then came the rub. Occupational and physical therapists came to my room with the wheelchair. They got me dressed in a matter of minutes, rolling me around in the bed. Once I was dressed, they put a lift pad under me. I could see that on the ceiling there was a track that moved from on top of the bed that could be moved to various places in the room.

I didn't know what a lift pad was until they put one under me when they got me dressed. The occupational therapist told me they were going to put me in my wheelchair. I was not opposed to this. However, I had not stood up or been upright for over a month. I had no idea what was about to happen.

The lift came down from the ceiling, and they strapped the four corners of my lift pad to it. Then the pad raised my body up out of the bed. So far, so good. The lift pad pulled my back up faster than my feet, putting me in the sitting position. Still okay. But then, things went south fast.

As the lift pad came up off the bed, I was feeling dizzy, and fear set in. No one had really talked about how I would feel sitting up for the first time. I was unprepared for the way my body would react to sitting up. Plus, my fear of heights did not serve me well as the lift raised me higher and higher off my bed.

These two factors caused me to yell in fear: "I want to go back down! I want to go back down!" When they saw my reaction, they consoled me as they lowered me back into the bed. "Jonathan, we will try again tomorrow. Don't worry. We won't do it for the rest of the day."

I had surprised myself. I didn't know I would react that way to sitting straight up and down. They explained that they had had similar reactions from other people their first time. I felt terrible. I had never reacted that way before.

One therapist explained that because my body had been flat for a month, my equilibrium was off, and that's why I became dizzy. I talked about my fear of heights. They promised not to raise me so high when we tried again the next day. I hoped this setback would not hinder my progress in rehab.

The Prayer of Faith

The power of faith is essential in the healing process, but even if we have faith, how do we express it? Like many saints who have come before us, we need to declare our faith to the Lord. One approach to healing in the Bible is the prayer of faith. This prayer allows us to express our faith to God and to come into His presence with our need of healing. As we speak our need to the Lord, we invite Him to do in our bodies exactly what He knows we need.

Our response to suffering and sickness must be to pray. In the prayer of faith, we also acknowledge our sickness and need for His miracle working power in us. James teaches on the power of the prayer of faith (Jas 5:13-16). He outlines how we can pray for our affliction. First, call for the elders of the church to pray over you. Combining your faith with the faith of the elders and their intercessory prayer over you is even more powerful. Second, the elders anoint you with oil in the name of the Lord.

Oil represents the Holy Spirit and shows how He is involved in healing your body. Pray in the name of the Lord, calling on the reputation and power of Jesus over your affliction. The Lord's name has great power because at His name, everything that has a name, every sickness, illness, disease, ailment, injury, disorder, and anything else must bow to the name of Jesus.

> I go for the biggest ask, the biggest request I have. I pray in faith
> and let the Lord do the rest.

Some people feel afraid when they hear the word *cancer* or some other name of their diagnosis. However, when the neurologists at Hershey Medical Center gave me the name for my injury, Acute Transverse Myelitis, I felt happy. Now that my injury had a name, it must bow to Jesus. It had no power any longer because it now fell under everything in creation that must bow to Him.

When we pray the prayer of faith, we must not have doubt among those who pray. James also speaks about praying without doubt (Jas 1:6-8). Why pray to Jesus to heal you if you have doubt that He can do it? Why would Jesus answer your prayer if you doubt His power? Instead, I go for the biggest ask, the biggest request I have. I pray in faith and let the Lord do the rest.

My First Power Wheelchair

After I had had about a week in the gym at McGee, several physical therapists measured me for a power wheelchair. There are different wheelchairs a paralyzed person can use, which range in difficulty to operate. The first wheelchair used buttons to control chair movement. These were the hardest for me because I didn't have any movement in my limbs.

The second wheelchair I tried had head controls. I controlled left and right by moving my head side to side. Three panels controlled the chair's movement by what I did with the panels. Tapping the left panel with my head made the chair turn left. Tapping the right with my head turned right. My struggle was to make the chair go and stop with the panel my head rested on. I did not have the needed strength and mobility to operate that chair.

My therapists didn't want to give me the option of the third chair because it is the hardest to learn to drive. Its operation is extremely difficult for most patients. It's called a Sip & Puff chair because you use a straw and a series of sips or puffs with varying intensity to go left, right, forward, backward, speed up, slow down, and stop. You need to leave time to slow down and stop before you hit something or someone.

They hesitate to give this wheelchair driving system to most patients because it can take up to a month to learn and intuitively drive the wheelchair without hurting the driver or anyone around them. Still, no other option had yet worked for me. So, they threw caution to the wind and let a legally blind quadriplegic get behind the straw.

Here's how the driving system worked. There were five steps of speed you could add to go faster and slower. To make the chair go forward and increase in speed one step at a time, I had to puff hard into the straw. To slow down or stop, I would sip softly. The faster you go, the longer it takes to sip until you stop.

There was an emergency stop in which you sip harder, but it still takes about a second to stop. To turn to the left, I had to sip softly. To turn right, I would puff softly. You can see how it could take up to a month for a person to learn the driving system, until it becomes second nature to the driver.

The therapist who trained me to drive had a "kill switch" to stop the wheelchair by turning it off if I made the wrong move. They set the wheelchair at the lowest speed at first for me to get the hang of it. It took me less than two weeks to learn and use the Sip & Puff driving system. The therapist always had the kill switch available but used it less and less. This is the wheelchair I have today.

With a straw in my mouth to drive, I can't talk to people while it is moving. People at church and everywhere may say hello to me or try to start a conversation, but I have to stop the chair before I can respond. I put the safety of others ahead of any conversation while I'm driving. Most people understand and just wave and say hello.

My Aids and Nurses

I had several aids at McGee who took care of me every day. On days I didn't have a shower, they gave me a bath. They also dressed me every morning. They helped me maintain a routine that kept me from just lying around all the time.

I remember one of my aids, a Muslim woman. A comedian named Jeff Dunham had skits he did with ventriloquism. One of his dummies was a skeleton Muslim that blew himself up and was a sort of afterlife creature. His catchphrase was, "Silence! I kill you."

She had never heard of him. Unwittingly, I started showing her some of his skits. I didn't realize until after the first one that they could be extremely offensive to Muslims. After the first skit, I realized with horror my mistake and begged her forgiveness. She laughed and said she thought they were hilarious. After that, we watched all the ones we could find on YouTube.

I am forever grateful to my aids and nurses—both then and now. They work very hard to take excellent care of me. They invest their time and themselves into my care. They have quickly become close friends. I thank God for each of them.

I have also had a lot of great nurses and doctors throughout this whole experience. One of my most memorable nurses was my Day Shift Nurse, Nurse Green. Every morning she would come into my room with all my meds. We would talk, and I would make her laugh.

But Nurse Green did not just giggle. She had this deep-from-the-toes belly laugh that made me laugh too. When I got my wheelchair, we used to play tricks on each other. She would be talking with her colleagues about this patient or that patient, and I would wheel up behind her real quiet. When she turned around, she would just about jump out of her skin. "Gotcha!" I would say, and promptly turn my wheelchair around while she chased me down the hall.

But Nurse Green was not to be outdone. I was getting occupational therapy, practicing driving my wheelchair one day, and she saw that I was coming down the hallway. She casually walked right out in front of me and stopped, staring me down, knowing that I would not be able to stop the wheelchair in time. I used the "kill switch" to stop the wheelchair. I have never been so afraid to hurt someone by accident! Of course, Nurse Green knew about the kill switch. I profusely apologized for almost "taking her out." She stood there and listened for a good minute or two. Then a big grin spread across her lips, "Gotcha!" My dismay over almost killing her turned into laughter.

I pulled the ultimate prank on her in my last week at MaGee. One of her pet peeves was when anyone sat at her station or touched anything on it. She went to do her med passes. I tried to enlist help from the other nurses and CNAs, but no one was brave enough to take me up on my offer.

When she wasn't looking, I went behind the nurses' station with my wheelchair and sat right in front of her desk. I put my wheelchair up in the air so it looked like I belonged there. Then I waited for the trap to be sprung.

She came around the corner and must not have noticed I was there. When she passed by her desk, I said, "Can I help you with anything today, Miss?" I really stirred the hornets' nest. I thought she was going to have a coronary. "No one gets behind my desk! You didn't touch anything, did you?"

I waited for that last sentence to sink in for a moment. She stopped. Then she smiled, "I guess you would be the only person I could trust not to touch my things." It was the last laugh we had together.

My Daily Routine

The next day, the therapists tried to put me in my wheelchair again. It went easier, and I was able to sit up in my wheelchair for a couple of hours. This would be a process to get back to where I was before my paralysis. I wondered how far I could go. I was feeling encouraged that this would not be forever.

Everyone wanted me to get into a normal routine. They tried to make it like my routine before my spinal cord injury. Routines are important because they get you moving for your day and productive. Once I was in my wheelchair, the occupational therapist wheeled me to the sink and mirror to comb my hair and brush my teeth. For the first couple of days while I got used to sitting up, that was as much as we did. After about four days of being there, I could sit in my wheelchair long enough to go to the gym for rehab.

Each day, after occupational and physical therapy, they brought me back to my room. For the first week, I got back into bed and spent the rest of the day watching TV. There wasn't much else to do. When I could stay in my wheelchair longer, there were activities to do and places I could go.

After dinner, if it was a day for my shower, they took me into a big, open shower. They had a shower bed I laid on for my shower. Then, they put me back in my bed. The worst part was my nights. Nurses woke me up every two hours to turn me onto my other side. Every day, all day long, I got turned if I wasn't in my wheelchair. This prevents skin breakdowns, but it interrupts my sleep patterns. Sometimes I still have trouble sleeping to this day.

Stretching in the Gym

MaGee Rehab Hospital had many helpful and fun parts to it. My favorite part was going to the gym every weekday. They had this huge gym for all kinds of rehab. It accommodated wheelchairs, stretching tables, weights, and an E-STIM (electrical stimulation) area. Most useful to me were the stretching tables and E-STIM area.

Every weekday, I would drive my chair to the gym for my rehab session. I had one in the morning with occupational therapy and one in the afternoon with physical therapy. In the morning, my occupational therapist stretched my arms and fingers. I have muscle contractions in my right elbow and right pointer finger.

Stretching me every day helped to keep these contractions from getting worse. A contraction is stiffness in joints or muscles. This stiffness can get worse if you don't do anything about it. From my evening showers to therapy, they did their best to stave off worsening contractions.

After my therapist stretched my arms, three times a week she put me on the E-STIM bike. E-STIM, or electrical stimulation, tried to make my muscles work. Electrical stimulation works the same way the nerves work in the body. Since I cannot move my muscles, the therapist placed electrical nodes at the proper places on them, whether on my arms or legs, and hooked them up to a machine that gave them electrical impulses. She then strapped my arms or legs to the machine and stimulated my muscles with the machine. It's the closest thing to using my muscles on my own. My arms or legs moved the bike. It looked like I was either pedaling a bike or doing the same motion with my arms.

In the afternoon, my physical therapist stretched out my legs. Sometimes we hooked me up to a lift and transferred to me to the stretching tables. She also used E-STIM, this time on my back. She applied the E-STIM nodules near my spine. When she activated the machine, my back muscles would tighten and straighten my neck up. I moved my head side to side and exercised my neck muscles.

Sometimes, we used a standing table. This was a table with straps on it. They transferred me from my wheelchair to the table, strapped me in, and slowly tilted the table until I was in a standing position. Of course, this took a couple of weeks to achieve. The therapists put me up at incremented angles until I was about 95 percent standing. This was my favorite of all the activities we did. It felt good to stand again.

Their goal was to maintain my muscles and bone structure. They kept me from getting stiff, my muscles from atrophying, and my bones from getting brittle or not being able to hold weight.

I enjoyed hanging out with my occupational and physical therapists. I had a great time talking off their ears during our sessions. We talked about everything from my profession as a minister to the things they liked to do. We got to know each other really well during those eight weeks. I was amazed of their tenacity and persistence every day, continuing to move my limbs despite my paralysis.

Be Persistent in Prayer

In Luke 18, Jesus teaches a parable about persistent prayer (vv. 1-8) and life between the promise of healing and its fulfillment. He refers to a widow who had an adversary who broke the law against her. He does not present any details, but we know that widows were part of the protected groups the Law provided for since society would not naturally take care of them.

Widows had no power in the social system. They couldn't buy property or even represent themselves in court—with some exceptions. They had no way to defend themselves. If they did not have a male family member who by chance cared for them, they had no recourse.

Whatever issue this widow Jesus refers to in Luke 18 comes to the unjust judge with, it is probably something the Law provided for her defense. However, this unjust judge decided not even to hear her case. So, she continues to come to him day after day and demands that he hear her case and rule in her favor as the Law requires. You may consider what she did pestering, but she had no other option. So, she kept coming and coming and coming.

Will people persist in prayer and faith if they don't get answers immediately?

The unjust judge finally decides that if he hears her case and gives her justice, she will leave him alone, and he will have some peace. He doesn't act justly. He acts out of selfishness. Jesus finishes the parable of the judge's decision to give her justice so that she won't bother him anymore. After the parable, He contrasts the unjust judge and God the Father. God is not unjust. One of His attributes is righteousness. When we cry out to Him day and night, over and over, He will answer our prayers.

Then Jesus asks a most interesting question, "When the Son of Man comes, will he find faith on the earth?" Why would Jesus ask this question when He teaches persistent prayer and faith? Perhaps what He's really asking is, "Will people persist in prayer and faith if they don't get answers immediately?"

You may have a question along the same lines. I pray for healing every day. I ask God to restore my nerves, muscles, and spinal cord. I want to walk again. Why do I have to ask every day when God has the power to immediately heal me?

"Healing delayed is not healing denied."

Is the answer "No" if he doesn't do it immediately? My grandma tells me, "Healing delayed is not healing denied." Daniel kept praying when he didn't receive a reply, only to find out from the angel Michael that God answered him, but His reply was delayed by warfare (Dan 10:12-13). I don't have all the answers. Our answers to prayer can be delayed in the spiritual realm. The Bible promises that God hears our prayers and answers them. Sometimes, His answer may be, "Not yet."

I think one of the reasons I have not yet been healed completely is that God wants to do it in front of a crowd of people like He did in the New Testament. He receives more glory from more people seeing the miracle and giving Him praise for it.

God may be strengthening and increasing your faith through the process of waiting—but waiting on the Lord is not easy. You need faith to trust that God will fulfill His promises. Can God do it in an instant? Absolutely! He does many times in the Gospels.

Perhaps He is growing our faith, preparing us for what it will be like when He completes the work of the promise. These are not excuses. Jesus clearly teaches in this parable that we must persist in prayer, praying the same requests persistently until God fulfills them.

I prefer to think that God is stretching my faith and my imagination for the day that He does fulfill the promise He gave. God is faithful, and He will do the work He has promised to do. He is the all-powerful Creator of this body. He can, and will, heal me and you. I can't explain why He hasn't done it yet, but He has given me no reason to stop trusting Him.

God is stretching my faith and my imagination for the day that He does fulfill the promise He gave.

Jesus calls us to remain persistent in prayer until we see the result that agrees with God's will. Praying for healing is praying in His will. Persist in prayer and faith. This is Jesus's expectation when He returns. As you wait for Him to complete what He has promised in your life and body, allow Him to strengthen your faith for your healing.

Jesus talks about faith that can move mountains (Matt 17:20). This faith brings God's promises to reality. He said faith as small as a mustard seed—one of the smallest seeds in the world—has big faith results. With just that amount of faith, you can move mountains.

God can use that kind of faith. He is not unjust like the judge. But we can lose hope over time. It is our inability to be patient and continue in faith, to trust in God's promises no matter how long it takes. Stay the course and increase your faith. God's promises never fail.

When I talk about the day of healing, am I speaking from experience more than doctrine? Not according to Jesus in this parable. His timing becomes my timing. Though Jesus doesn't tell us why we must persist in prayer, He does tell us to persist. He doesn't enumerate God's reasons why He doesn't answer our prayers immediately. He calls us to have faith and to wait for Him. Don't stop praying for your healing. It's coming! Even when our present reality confuses us, we can still believe in God's unfailing promises.

"I'm So Cold"

I remember the beginning days in the rehab hospital. I knew I couldn't feel the difference between cold and hot, but I always felt so cold when I woke up. It didn't make any sense. Was my brain interpreting my nerve pain as a temperature?

I asked for more and more blankets. They would only give me so many, and they wouldn't change how I felt. I thought I was freezing. Maybe it was psychological. Even having at least one blanket on helped me think I was not as cold.

I know what it's like to get mixed signals in my head. I have had times when, if I didn't look down at my legs, I thought they were falling off the bed. Yet when the neurologists had tested me for the ability to tell where my limbs were and which way they were pointed, I always knew what was happening.

Spinal cord injuries don't make sense. Between the neuropathies and the other challenges your body and mind face, they can cause great confusion. It's the strangest thing sending signals to your body to move just as you always have, yet your body does not obey. I can think about something all I want, but it does not change my body's response.

I can know I'm not cold, but that's the only way my brain can interpret what my nerves are telling it. There were times before and after sleep when I could have sworn I was moving my toes and feet … but they weren't moving.

If—and this was rare—I had a caretaker who didn't seem to understand my pain or treat me well, we imagined that they could switch places with me. It wasn't vindictive. I just wanted them to understand what I was going through. Perhaps that would give them just a bit more empathy.

Putting yourself in another person's shoes is not easy. It requires a little bit of imagination. You must imagine how they feel, what they're going through, and how life is different for them. I can't say I completely have this gift, but I try to do it as a minister. If you struggle to imagine what someone else is feeling, just ask that person questions to gain perspective and understanding.

Getting My Voice Back

While at MaGee, they assigned a speech therapist to me. This therapist wanted to work on my eating, breathing, and speaking.

First, it was time to talk again. I felt elated about getting my voice back. There's nothing better than for a preacher to use his or her voice.

Until that point, my trach was cuffed, stopping the air from my lungs from going through my vocal cords. The speech therapist took the air out of the balloon over my trachea. It was a strange feeling, like pressure being released in the middle of my neck. When the balloon was empty, she told me to speak.

At first, nothing came out. I continued to try speaking. She advised me not to push too hard since I had been silent for six weeks. As I relaxed, air passed through my vocal cords. I finally heard noises. I sounded like a bad impression of Donald Duck. My voice would get stronger over time.

Next, she wanted me to start weaning, the process of breathing without the vent. She introduced me to a Passy-Muir Valve (named after its inventor)). This little device was placed over the trach hole in the tubing and made it hard for me to breathe out through my trach. I could breathe in through my trach but had to breathe out through my mouth and nose. It teaches a person to breathe in small increments.

To use the PMV, the therapist put my trach cuff down. I had a cuffed trach that closed my lungs off when I swallow. There was a little balloon where the opening went into my lungs over the epiglottis, a muscle that kept me from aspirating (getting water and food particles in my lungs).

Eating and Drinking Again

Finally, the speech therapist wanted to help me to eat and drink again. Until now, we had relied on my G-tube for food, water, and medicine. It had been about eight weeks since I could eat and drink.

Before I could try, I had to take a video swallow test. This would help the therapist determine whether there was output in my epiglottis or not. The epiglottis is the muscle that protects your lungs when you eat or drink. It closes over your trachea when you eat and drink, but it opens when you talk.

I went to an X-ray machine hooked up to video equipment. We could watch the process of eating from chewing to swallowing food. Her trained eyes were looking at my epiglottis. It was working fine after several tests. She started me on easier things to swallow, like yogurt. Then she moved on to breads, and I even got to have a piece of a doughnut.

My epiglottis functioned the way it should, and I could eat and drink again. She wanted me to begin with puréed foods. These are terrible. I couldn't find anything I liked. Everything tastes different than it should when it is not puréed. I refused at first to eat these puréed foods, but she told me she could not move me to solid food if I did not try.

> I survived on these soups for one week before she allowed me to eat solid food again. That was one of the best days since I had become a quadriplegic.

I finally found that chicken noodle soup and tomato soup taste about the same either way. I survived on these soups for one week before she allowed me to eat solid food again. That was one of the best days since I had become a quadriplegic.

My First Trach Change

When the doctors at Hershey Medical Center installed my trach, they never told me it needed to be changed every month. At MaGee, six weeks after my tracheostomy surgery, they changed it and checked to see how my neck was healing from the surgery. I had no idea what was about to happen to me. This experience has scarred me psychologically to this day.

A familiar face and an unfamiliar one darkened the door of my room. My respiratory therapist for that day and either an ENT (Ear, Nose, Throat Doctor) or pulmonologist came in talking with one another.

The respiratory therapist did not say they were changing my trach. He only talked about maintenance. So, I was unprepared for what happened next. They loosened the ties around my neck and pulled my trach out. This was not unfamiliar because they did this during my regular trach care. Without any other warning, however, the respiratory therapist pulled the trach out of my neck! I was in full panic mode. *Could I breathe without that?* Worse was the image stuck in my mind forever—a lovely piece of bloody plastic with pieces of skin stuck to it dangling in the air.

I was horrified. *Is it supposed to look like that?* I would find out later that it's not. All the time they had this out, probably about half a minute or so, I'm still wondering if I can breathe. The doctor shone a light in the hole in my neck and said, "Looks like it's healing nicely" (I'd find out later he was probably wrong).

Then came another plastic trach. I was smart enough to have closed my eyes by now. I didn't try to breathe because I didn't know what to do. Then came the pain as the respiratory therapist pushed the new trach into the hole, wiped the lubricant around the hole, and tied the trach ties to keep the trach firmly in place.

I kept my eyes closed, and they left the room. I was left with pain in my neck muscles every time I swallowed, coughed, and even moved my neck in certain ways. Later that day I talked through the experience with the respiratory therapist. He didn't realize I had no idea it needed to be changed regularly.

One of the things I have learned in my medical experiences is that I must ask questions of medical professionals so I feel prepared for these new experiences. I wish they would think from the patient's perspective and realize that these things are new, and the patient doesn't know what to expect.

To this day when I have a trach change, that image is what I see when my eyes are closed. I focus my thoughts on Jesus and His peace, and He gives me peace and strength to endure the trach change. In the middle of my fear and anxiety, I concentrate on God's goodness. Only a few times I have failed to focus on Jesus instead of my trach change. Like Peter watching the wind and waves as he walked on water to Jesus, those trach changes don't go as well.

Today, every time a trach change is scheduled, I email and call a select group of prayer warriors to intercede for me and come alongside me spiritually before the change. Their prayers mean a world of difference for me. For at least the last six months, I have had complete peace before and during my trach changes. I used to obsess about them, think about them up to a week before they happened. Prayer has made the difference for me.

Praying When You Don't Understand

When you don't understand what's happening to you, this is the best time to pray. Talking to God about your experience, what doesn't make sense, and what you don't know how to handle is the best use of your time. When I don't understand what's happened to me, crying out to God is both comforting and encouraging.

I experience a familiar place as I talk to God. It comforts me because it's familiar and because He answers me. I can talk to Him about my feelings and experiences. He understands. I don't always get a response from Him or get an explanation but being in God's presence gives me a sense of security in my world of curiosities.

Praying when I don't understand what's happened to me also encourages me. God's sweet presence gives me a feeling that even though I don't know what to do, God has me in the palm of His hand. He won't drop me or let me go. I trust in His power and presence. Sometimes His answers give me more questions. No matter His response, though, I know He remains in control.

When you need reassurance, understanding, and answers, there's no better place to be than in God's presence. He guides you and understands the insecurity you feel. I don't need to talk all the time. Just being in God's presence is enough. I place my trust in Him. I lay my insecurity and fear about my future in His hands, and He unburdens me. He can do that for you.

God's Peace Overcomes Anxiety

As I mentioned earlier, because my tracheostomy was not properly done at Hershey, my trach is not centered on my neck but is to the right, which makes it harder to change every month. About six months after the ENT fixed it when I came home, it has fully healed, and trach changes have been easier.

My muscles when I'm anxious during the trach change tighten as the old trach is pulled out of my neck. I cough and spasm when the new trach is put in my neck. It takes less than ten seconds for the procedure. Jesus is teaching me how to take my anxious thoughts captive. I give them over to Him and ask for His peace.

When you feel fear or anxiety, you must surrender these enemies of your faith to God. He can give you peace in a world full of anxiety and fear. It's hard to surrender. Despite my surrender, my muscles still react to the change. But I receive God's peace as only He can calm me down.

Paul speaks of God's peace that passes understanding (Phil 4:7). How right he was. I don't always receive His peace well, but even a little peace from Him is enough. We seek other ways to distract ourselves from pain and suffering, but God's peace is the best solution. He takes away our fears and anxieties, and we receive His perfect, unexplainable peace to face our circumstances.

Prepare for War

How do you pray for your affliction? Do you have a group of prayer warriors and intercessors? Form a group of people who minister to you through prayer.

Pray in faith without doubt. Ask Jesus to take away your fears and worries. Pray every day for your healing and be persistent.

Chapter 4
Trust through Dark Times

"Even though I walk through the valley of the deep shadow of gloom and death, I will not fear evil because you are with me."
(Psalm 23:4)

It is often in our darkest times that we give up or seek other remedies, but this is the time we must turn everything over to God, keep faith in Him and His promises. We need faith the most when we don't understand what's happening to us and when our circumstances weigh heavily upon us.

How can we have faith during the struggle between God's promises and their fulfillment? We seek answers and understanding. We want to give up and give in. There's no relief from the pain. There's no comfort for our suffering. We turn to other things like medicine and daily distractions.

We feel no reprieve. Our suffering from our affliction gets sharper and deeper. If you don't cry out to God, seek His presence, and continue to trust in Him in these times, who can you cry out to? No one else understands like Jesus does. In these times, hold on to God because He never fails. Things were about to change from the hospital and the rehab hospital. It was time for me to fly out into the world. MaGee Rehabilitation Hospital prepared me for what I was about to walk into. Jesus knows how to prepare us for the next step.

Finding New Homes

The last couple of weeks at MaGee, we planned my next steps. We had to find a skilled nursing facility with respiratory therapists. Only three or four places in the state could handle my care.

I couldn't go home with my parents because my dad was still working at the time. My parents could not guarantee they could take care of me if we didn't have nursing. However, I knew it wasn't easy for them to visit me when I was farther away from them. A trip to Philly was around four to four and a half hours.

Where I would go next depended on whether a place had an open bed and could take care of me. My parents checked out a place in Mechanicsburg called Fox Subacute Nursing Home that seemed to check all the boxes. People from Fox came to MaGee with promo materials talking about respiratory therapists and how they knew they could handle my care. My mom and dad took time to visit the facility to see how they cared for the patients there; they went there with MaGee being the standard of care. At MaGee, CNAs and staff pushed wheelchairs through the halls and took such great care of their patients that my parents wanted the same care for me.

When my folks visited Fox, they saw CNAs and nurses taking the time to talk to the patients, wheel them around in their wheelchairs, and attend activities with them. It looked like a good place to send me, so they came back telling me they thought they had found a place. We settled on moving me to Mechanicsburg, which was closer to my parents from Philadelphia. It wouldn't be as long a drive for them, and it felt like I was moving in the right direction toward my parents. I stayed at MaGee until my place was ready at Fox, just before Christmas.

My Accommodations at Fox

I arrived late at night at Fox in Mechanicsburg. It looked like they were the right place for me. I had an air mattress and a vent machine like the one I used at MaGee. They even arranged for me to have the same straw-like call bell system. They surprised me when they arranged all this for me.

My mom arrived about the same time. She unloaded my belongings and put them in the closet for me. She stayed for a while to talk with me and pray with me in this new place. We were stepping out into the world. There were no more rehab hospitals.

When my mom left on December 21, I felt positive about the move. We didn't know how long I would be in a skilled nursing home. At least they seemed to know about the equipment a quadriplegic needed. I watched some TV before I went to bed. I hoped they had activities I could do and that I could meet more of the staff and residents the next day.

My First Day

My first morning at the Mechanicsburg home was a rude awakening. The CNA brought my breakfast in, set it down on the table in front of me, and said, "I'll be back in half an hour to collect your tray."

I stared at her in disbelief, "Who is going to feed me?"

"I don't have time to feed you. I've got other things to do."

"Then how am I going to eat?"

"I don't know." And with that she left me to my own devices. She returned in half an hour with a surprised look on her face, "Why didn't you eat your breakfast?"

"I'm a quadriplegic. Do you know what that means?"

"Yes."

It was as if the dots did not connect for her. So, I made it very clear: "I cannot move my hands or my arms. I have no way to eat food in front of me without help. That's why I'm in a skilled nursing facility. If only I could find a skilled medical professional to help me."

"Well, I guess we'll have to figure something out for the rest of your meals then." Without another word she took my tray and left. I was happy I still had my feeding tube and was receiving enough nourishment through it.

Find Comfort in God

We face dark times when there is no comfort from caregivers and other people who don't understand our situation. Most people just don't have experiences like I'm sharing in this chapter. I went from a modern marvel of a rehab hospital to a place where I was ill-treated by a facility that had promised great things.

In his most biographical letter to the Corinthians, Paul opens by praising the God of all comfort (2 Cor 1:3-5). Paul suffered much as he ministered for Jesus during his missionary journeys. He understood pain and affliction.

No one can comfort you in your suffering like Jesus; He suffered more than anyone in human history because He bore all the suffering of humanity and suffers the pain of seeing us go through our affliction. He knows how you feel. He's been there. You can always go to Him for comfort; He walks with you in your suffering.

God's grace and presence comfort us. The Holy Spirit blesses us with His presence in us. We can come to God in our weakness, and He makes us strong. King David also knew God's comfort; he writes in Psalm 23 that he found comfort in the guidance of God's rod and staff (v. 4).

Jesus also provides saints and people to comfort us. The ministry of hospitality flourished in the Early Church, and they knew how to take care of one another. We can turn to saints who God provides for comfort. God ministers through those who have endured afflictions and suffering as we do now. They understand with experience some of the suffering we face.

Turn to God and to those He provides in times of pain and suffering. When you're in a dark place, you need the encouragement that God's people provide. Read Scripture that encourages you. The Scriptures serve as the light to guide your way to God's peace that passes understanding (Phil 4:7). Pray in God's presence and ask Him for His strength and peace. In your darkest times, there is always His light. God sends people to brighten your day who truly care about you.

My Physical Therapist

Two or three times a week at Fox, a physical therapist would come to see me. Like the physical therapists at MaGee, she ranged my arms, stretched my limbs, hands, and fingers, and tried to progress my training. We discussed sitting on the edge of my bed and other accommodations I needed.

I talked about my power wheelchair at MaGee. Unfortunately, they had no such wheelchairs, but she tried to do everything in her power to keep me mobile. They had a wheelchair I was willing to try. It was stiff, and I needed an aid to push the wheelchair. If the staff were too busy to feed me three meals a day, they certainly couldn't push me around the facility.

The first time my physical therapist put me in this wheelchair, I tried to sit in it for a couple of hours. I achieved that goal, but my body couldn't take it. She asked me to try again the next day. It wasn't any better. I gave it a week, but I wasn't making any progress.

In a place where I knew within a week the wheelchair would not work for me, that I needed more specialized care, and that I would need to advocate for myself like never before, my physical therapist was a bright spot. She encouraged me and tried harder than anyone else there to keep me in the same condition I had been at MaGee.

Embrace Positive Change

When you're dealing with long-term affliction, any positive change is a reason to thank the Lord, praise Him, and celebrate His goodness. Thank God for the three or four little-to-no nerve pain days I have each month. Neuropathy doesn't make any sense, but I praise God it's not completely unbearable.

I praise God when I receive a positive report from the doctors. I thank Him when I can go on vacation to Florida or sit in my wheelchair for eight hours or more. I give God the glory and credit for new feeling in my body.

I thank God for pain. Why? Because if I didn't feel pain, I wouldn't know I could feel at all. Most quadriplegics have no feeling from their sensory nerves. They don't know if a person is touching them other than that painful spasms result from that touch. I praise God because I can feel touch. It's not 100 percent, but it's something.

How do you respond to positive changes in your condition? We need to give God the highest praise because He's worthy of it and because He's the reason positive change happens. God doesn't have to do something for you to deserve praise from your lips. He doesn't have to heal you for you to glorify Him. The Bible says if we don't praise Him, the rocks will cry out in our place (Hab 2:11; Luke 19:40).

In prison, Paul and Silas worshiped and praised the Lord (Acts 16:25). Going through dark times does not give us an excuse to not praise our Creator and Lord. We should praise God even more when we are in our dark times. He is with us wherever we go and in whatever we struggle with. Everyone may abandon us as they did Job, but God remains with us.

The good times and positive changes are a welcome reprieve from the suffering and pain we normally feel. Embrace the good times, the positive changes in your health and life, and praise God for them. Even in the dark times when pain is unbearable, seek God's presence and use that time to pray, even if only for the pain to subside.

Entering God's Presence

David said God's presence was always with him (Ps 139:7-12). Some people may want to be alone occasionally, to not have God looking over their shoulder. But oh, what a blessing it is to know that if no one else is with us, God remains here with us.

In the dark times, we can cry out to God, and He is right there. It's comforting to know that He never leaves us or forsakes us (Heb 13:5). When we cry out in the darkness, His light is with us. He is the God of all comfort (2 Cor 1:3). The Holy Spirit is with you, and Jesus understands better than anyone else your suffering, pain, and loneliness.

Jesus endured loneliness for at least the last week of His life. We think of His suffering on the Cross as the only time He endured such pain, agony, and loneliness. He cried out, "My God, my God, why have you forsaken me" (Matt 27:46)? Consider Jesus's prayers in the Garden of Gethsemane. His disciples could not even stay awake to pray with Him (Matt 26:40). The only person who the Gospels mention that may have had any empathy for Jesus was the woman with the alabaster jar who anointed Him for burial (Matt 26:6-13; Mark 14:3-5; Luke 7:37-39; John 12:1-8).

Throughout His ministry, even Jesus's disciples often could not understand Him or His teaching. But Jesus was never alone. His regular practice before the rigors of ministry was to find secluded places to pray and commune with the Father. He taught us by example that we can always run into the loving arms of the Father.

Do you take advantage of those lonely times of solitude and seclusion to meet with Jesus? When I can't sleep in the morning or at night, I spend some of that time in prayer, enjoying the Lord's presence. Do you see times of silence and loneliness as opportunities to commune with Jesus?

Languishing in a Dark Place

I was ready to move away from Fox by the end of the first week. My room only had a few lights and was dark, even with the lights on. I rang my call bell every couple of hours to reposition my body and get a drink. Apparently, this was too much for the aids and nurses on each shift to handle.

They scolded me for ringing my call bell so much. Several times after ringing it, I waited for up to three hours for someone to respond and come into my room to help me. Most of the overworked and unhelpful staff probably thought I was an annoyance.

The facility psychologist visited me after a week or two. She asked me questions and took notes. The questions asked if I was depressed or suicidal. I asked her why she was asking about depression and suicidal thoughts.

She said she had to ask about my mental state. I was joking around with her, smiling and chuckling. I asked her, "Would a depressed or suicidal patient be smiling, laughing, and joking around?"

"I'm referring to your overall mental state, not what you're doing right now."

"But doesn't my jovial mood show you I'm not depressed or suicidal?"

"I still have to ask these questions. It's part of my state-mandated job," she countered.

I smiled, "How would I do it?"

"Do what?"

"Commit suicide. I can't use my arms, hands, legs, or feet. Even if I was suicidal, which I'm not, how would I commit suicide?"

She stared at me for a while. The question didn't seem to register with her. "It's about your mental state, not whether or not you would carry it out."

I continued, "But what danger am I to myself if I can't do what I'm thinking of doing? How does a suicidal mental state hurt me? I would just make myself miserable."

> If I was breathing, even if with the help of a ventilator, Jesus still had work for me to do.

She refused to acknowledge my reasoning. I argued that I was not depressed or suicidal. I didn't know what she was writing for answers. Then she told me she was prescribing me Xanax. She didn't explain what Xanax was for. She didn't tell me the dose either. My days became darker and darker, but Jesus kept me alive.

I was convinced that if I was breathing, even if with the help of a ventilator, Jesus still had work for me to do. Despite my dark surroundings, I held on to that belief. I often prayed and asked Jesus how to fulfill my call as a minister in this condition. I asked Him to show me the way to glorify Him while paralyzed. I prayed fervently for my healing and for a way out of this situation at Fox.

Facing Challenges to Your Faith

We need faith every day. It fuels our hope. You need faith more than ever in the dark times. Satan designs these dark times to drain your faith and hope. David didn't talk about faith in the high spiritual times of God's blessing. He expressed his faith "In the valley of the shadow of death" (Ps 23:4).

The psalmists spoke in faith and talked about hope when they were in trouble. Faith works every day, but it works best when fear, doubt, and every negative emotion threaten to pierce our souls. Faith gets us through the uncertainties of life. It's the medicine our divine Doctor ordered to combat our reality and our emotions. It gives us certainty in uncertain times.

In the dark times, cry out to Jesus even more. Ask Him to increase your faith. Believe He has your best days ahead. Don't let the devil get you down. Don't let him win. Dark times are places the Lord can use to strengthen your faith muscles.

How else would God strengthen our faith and character? We see adversity as a negative thing in our lives, but God sees it as a way to increase our faith, build our character, and teach us to run to Him when we can't handle our surroundings and situations. James tells us to "consider it pure joy when you face trials of various kinds" (Jas 1:2).

Are Christians masochists who should learn to enjoy the pain? No. We learn to see God's hand in the middle of our trials, helping us to grow. We know He is working out all things together for our good (Rom 8:28). When you read that verse in context, Paul talks next about God's designed plan to conform us to the image of Christ (vv. 29-30).

We can have joy when we face trials, pain, and suffering because we know God's hand is working behind these afflictions for His glory in us. Knowing that God has greater things for us on the other side of our affliction, our mountain, and our suffering gives us reason for joy. We can't see the end from the beginning, but in the middle, we can anticipate God's blessings.

Train yourself to think of the glories and blessings that Jesus will bring when you reach the end of your suffering. Imagine what your healing will look like. Seek Jesus's presence and dwell in the shadow of His wings (Ps 17:8; 36:7; 53:7). Go to the Lord in your suffering instead of seeking frivolous means of distraction. Read Scripture. Meditate on God's goodness. Seek ways to minister to others and allow the light of Jesus's glory in you to shine. My mom did that for me at Fox's in my dark moments

My Mom's Visits

My parents have been examples of Jesus and biblical training. They have always shown me God's godliness, service, and love. This has been no different through my affliction. My dad was working, so he visited me on the weekends and came when he could. My mom came to visit me regularly at Fox, usually once a week. The staff was so busy that they sometimes did not take care of my needs. Mom came a time or two and said I stank so bad she couldn't stand it. More than once, she gave me a bath, and let them know how badly I stank.

When she was visiting me after a couple of weeks, she couldn't keep me awake long enough to have a two-minute conversation. I kept falling asleep again. She wanted to know why I was sleeping so much. I hadn't realized that I was falling asleep so much. I told her about the psychologist who came to visit me that week. She asked me a bunch of questions about being depressed and suicidal because I was a quadriplegic.

I told her I was not depressed but happy to be alive. Then it dawned on me, "Mom, I'm pretty sure she prescribed a medicine for my 'depressed and suicidal mood' that I argued with her about." My mom would have none of that. She wanted to know what was happening.

We finally got ahold of the psychologist. She told us she prescribed 75 mg of Xanax per day. That's why I was sleeping all the time! My mom was ready to fly off the handle. When we asked the reason for the evaluation, her insistence upon declaring me depressed and suicidal, we finally discovered the issue. We couldn't believe the reason for the evaluation. Every couple of hours I rang my bell because I needed a drink or repositioned. When you can't move your limbs or your body, you go stir crazy. When you can move, even in small increments, you don't think about how much your body needs to move.

Because I used my call bell every couple hours, apparently this was too often for the staff to handle. They ignored my call bell regularly, once or twice up to three hours. So, they decided that if I slept more often—hence the Xanax—I would not bother them as much with ringing for their help.

Your Affliction Won't Last Forever

When we live through our affliction, we think it will never end, but that's not how the Bible characterizes affliction. People who endured afflictions their whole life experienced the healing and freedom of Jesus. The man born blind in John 9 experienced

Jesus's healing touch. At the point of having thirty-eight years of suffering under his belt, this man heard Jesus ask him, "Do you want to be healed?" (John 5:6).

> **Embrace this: your affliction has an expiration date.**

Believe it or not, it's possible to get so used to our afflictions that we stop seeking Jesus for healing. We accept it as our "new normal." During the COVID-19 pandemic, this became a phrase news pundits threw around. I hated that phrase then, and I hate it now. I don't care how long I endure this paralysis; I will never accept it as "normal."

The Bible teaches us to be persistent in prayer (Luke 18:1-8). The widow who sought the unjust judge for a favorable verdict never stopped. She never gave up. She wore the judge out with her constant pleas for justice. God is not an unjust judge. Every good gift we receive comes from Him (Jas 1:17). We must not get a wrong view of God. He is on our side.

Embrace this: your affliction has an expiration date. You will not live in pain forever. Your suffering will cease. If not in this life, it will end in heaven. John sees a revelation fulfilled in Isaiah when he repeats the words of Isaiah's prophecy in Revelation that God will wipe away every tear from their eyes (Rev 7:17; Isa. 25:8). God will turn your mourning into dancing (Ps 38:11), and joy comes in the morning (30:5).

The wise preacher of Ecclesiastes says there is a time for everything (Eccl 3:1). If you cannot see the light at the end of the tunnel, look up to heaven, for your redemption draws near (Luke 21:28). Job suffered greatly for a time, but at the end of the book, God doubles his blessings. He was honest about his feelings and not understanding God's purpose in his affliction, but the Bible declares that Job never sinned in all he said (Job 1:22; 2:10).

God Gives You Grace

When Paul talks about his extraordinary vision of heaven in 2 Corinthians 12, he also says that the visions were so great that Satan harassed him with a "thorn in the flesh" to keep him from becoming conceited (2 Cor 12:7-8). Scholars are divided on what this thorn in the flesh was. Some point to an eye disease and others to his sufferings on his missionary journeys.

Whatever it was, Paul saw it as an obstacle in his life that would help keep him humble. He prayed three times for God to remove it, but God chose not to do that. Instead, He gave Paul sufficient grace to endure his affliction (2 Cor 12:8-9). God will give you His strength as you endure your affliction. God's power is complete in your weakness.

God ministers to others through our faithfulness in our affliction. Remain faithful to Him, putting your faith in His sovereign control of your affliction. What would your pain and suffering be like without trusting Jesus for relief and comfort? He is with you, and that is more than enough.

Join the Hall of Faith

Hebrews 11, the faith chapter, brings me encouragement. As I read about the saints who went before me and faced many challenges, I hope that I may live as a modern saint full of such faith. The writer of Hebrews says about the great heroes of faith "of whom the world was not worthy" (Heb 11:38). They suffered many things and did not receive the fulfillment of God's promises to them in their lifetime.

I hope my faith will measure up to even half of theirs. Faith is not blind, as some suggest. Hope and faith work together to see into God's promises and to trust in their fulfillment. We hope for what we do not experience yet. Our faith reinforces that hope. Though we have not yet seen God's fulfillment of our healing, our faith assures us it will be our reality (Heb 11:1).

When you choose to put your faith and hope in God's future for you instead of your current reality, you join the 'Hall of Faith' in Hebrews 11. I want to be known as a man of faith, not for my own reputation or because of my pride, but to be known by God in my pursuit of Him—and to live as an example to others. May we all have the faith that pleases God and brings us His reward, greater than the riches of this world in life.

Jesus has revealed himself to me in powerful and intimate ways as He walks with me through this affliction. He has proven himself to me over and over. I want to measure up to my big brothers and sisters in the faith. I hope I do not let Jesus down in the middle of my affliction when I suffer in the dark times and the wastelands between lush gardens.

Finally Free

I lived at Fox in Mechanicsburg for about 8 weeks. We got me out of there as soon as possible. They were milking the Social Security system for as much money as they could get out of me being at their facility.

My freedom day came when they let me go. Paramedics came and transferred me from the air mattress to their litter. As they wheeled me out of that room, the psychologist had the gall to say, "If you ever need a place to stay, just let us know."

I replied, "Okay. Goodbye." My mom knows I never say goodbye. Anytime I part company with someone, I reply with, "See you later." I wasn't coming back. It was the first time I ever felt abused by a facility. I never wanted to see that place again—and I never looked back.

It's healthy to not want to return to your dark times and places. Israel kept comparing the wilderness to their slavery in Egypt. Every time they encountered difficulty, they wanted to go back to Egypt. Even when they were in the Promised Land, they wanted to make alliances with Egypt, but God was firmly against them going back to the house of slavery.

> It's healthy to not want to return to your dark times and places.

God does not want you to go back to your dark places. Even if they were brighter spots than the darkness you face now, God wants freedom for you. Paul writes, "It was for freedom that Christ set us free (Gal 5:1). Don't turn back. Move forward and press on toward the goal of health and healing. You will find that in Jesus.

I endured my first painful experience of darkness and loneliness in that facility in Mechanicsburg. They told me they knew how to take care of quadriplegics, but when I arrived, it was the darkest experience I've had while being a quadriplegic. Fox was not the end of my story, though. God was writing more chapters. He's writing more chapters in your story, too.

God Gets the Glory

It's difficult to grasp what Paul says about affliction. He describes everything he suffered as an apostle of Christ (2 Cor 11:23-29). After he lists his sufferings as an apostle, then Paul talks about his vision of paradise (12:2-5). Paul also talks about his sufferings as "light and momentary afflictions" (4:17). Our afflictions are nothing compared to the glory of eternity. Paul calls affliction "an eternal weight of glory." We don't focus on our transitory afflictions. Paul says to focus on the things that are unseen, placing our faith in God's grace (v. 18). Before Paul comes to this conclusion about his afflictions, he characterizes them in stark ways, as his feeling pressed hard on every side, but not crushed, along with further suffering (vv. 8-11).

God ministers to others through you. He does not receive glory from your affliction but from the faith you model before others and the encouragement and inspiration you give others as you faithfully serve Him. God receives glory when you share the small steps toward healing that increase people's faith and brings God glory. You can be a powerful witness of God's glory in you. God's light shines through you as you follow Him (Phil 2:15-18).

Despite all Paul suffered, he ran his race and pressed on toward the prize of the upward call in Christ Jesus (Phil 3:13-14). Like Paul, during our afflictions, we place our faith in God with eternal purpose and vision. Don't focus on your suffering. Think of the greater glory you give God during your affliction.

Light at the End of the Tunnel

Dark times do come to an end. The darkness I experienced at Fox in Mechanicsburg lasted a couple of months. They may be the best thing since sliced bread for people needing kidney dialysis, but if you are a quadriplegic, don't go there.

My parents kept hunting for a better place. They found a place in Hamburg, PA called The Laurel Center. It seemed a lot like my rehab hospital. They even had a therapy place downstairs. Hamburg was about thirty minutes from my parsonage in Shillington.

So, on February 12, 2014, my dad greeted me at this new place when I arrived by ambulance escort. He helped me put my things in my closet and stayed with me for a while. Mom was at work in her tax office. The staff seemed nice and wanted to hear all about me. So began the next chapter of my story.

Prepare for War

Your faith shines in the darkness and overcomes it. You can stand the tests of your affliction because of your strong faith. It cannot be defeated by time or circumstance.

What increases your faith and inspires you in dark times? How can you stand for Jesus and be a witness of His grace in your affliction? What can you share with others to inspire them to keep their faith?

Chapter 5
Wait for Your Healing

"But those who wait on the Lord shall renew their strength. They shall ascend with wings like eagles. They shall run and not be weary. They shall walk and not faint" (Isaiah 40:31).

The Gospels overwhelmingly show that Jesus's healings took immediate effect, but what if you do not receive healing after praying for it? Many people today find themselves between God's promises for healing and their fulfillment in their lives now.

These people are in the same boat as me, having doctors tell them their condition is irreversible. They are stuck with their affliction. Until the Lord heals them, they are in a waiting period. We must learn from this waiting time. How do we wait on the Lord? What do we do in the meantime?

Do you think that by calling this a waiting period that that means you don't have to do anything? Is this a time to wallow in self-pity, just do the bare minimum, or make up your own plans and agendas? No, the waiting time is for spiritual growth and active participation in God's will for your life; it provides an opportunity to serve others.

Facing Interruptions

Jairus was desperate. His daughter was lying at home sick and at the precipice of death. Only fathers understand the love Jairus had for his daughter. He would do anything. As a synagogue ruler, he had heard about Jesus, but it was a taboo to support Him. Jairus didn't care, though; he needed a miracle, and Jesus was rumored to do miracles.

So, he found out where Jesus was and went to Him. He knew Jesus could heal. He was so desperate for his daughter's healing that we don't know what he believed. Jesus can heal even if we don't believe in His power. He found Jesus, begging Him to come and heal his daughter, and Jesus agreed to come with Jairus to his house.

Jairus managed to do what he came to do—to get Jesus to come to his house where his daughter lay—but something terrible happened on the way. Some woman snuck up to Jesus and touched His outer garment and was changed forever. Her issue of blood dried up, and she was healed of her twelve-year infirmity.

Jairus didn't know how to get Jesus back on track to his house. Jesus took time for this woman. When every second counted, Jesus delayed by calling the woman out and making her tell the whole crowd her story. In that moment, Jairus did not concern himself with how many people the woman made unclean in the crowd.

How could this Healer delay any longer? Sure enough, people from his household delivered the news Jairus was dreading. His daughter had passed away when this interruption happened. His heart stopped at the news. Everything around him paused.

As the little faith he had sank into despair, Jesus walked over and whispered in his ear, "Don't doubt. Just believe." Believe what? Nothing was left. His heart died with his little girl. The embers of hope were growing cold. Perhaps Jesus wrapped His arm around him and gently pushed him toward his hopeless house.

When they arrived at Jairus' house, Jesus surprisingly said, "The girl is not dead. She is sleeping." This was met with laughter by the professional mourners. For some unknown reason, Jairus did not laugh. He silently fanned hope on the embers, and they glowed.

He realized all that Jesus did in that interruption. If He could heal a woman with a twelve-year sickness, maybe He could do something for his twelve-year-old daughter. Twelve is the number of completion; could He bring completion into his life now at the point of such grief? Why would Jesus encourage him if there was no hope? Jairus hung on to that little bit of hope.

Jesus gathered Peter, James, John, and the girl's parents and went into the house. Jairus stared at his daughter's lifeless body. It took everything within him to hope that Jesus could do something. He watched as Jesus calmly took his daughter's hand. He whispered something in her ear, and Jairus caught, "Little girl arise."

To his amazement, his daughter's eyes opened, and color returned to her pale, lifeless skin. His wife embraced him as their daughter arose from the bed and walked around the room. Jesus told them to get her something to eat. The interruption only mattered to teach the girl's parents Jesus's power.

> I had to realize that my relationship with Him—not the pastoral ministry I had been doing—was my purpose. I found my identity in Him instead of in my worth as a pastor. And then He gave me ministry in unconventional ways.

Our affliction interrupts our lives. Mine stopped my pastoral ministry ... or so I thought. When I lay in that hospital bed wondering if I no longer had a purpose, God continued my ministry at the Laurel Center. I had to realize that my relationship with Him—not the pastoral ministry I had been doing—was my purpose. I found my identity in Him instead of in my worth as a pastor. And then He gave me ministry in unconventional ways.

What is God doing in your interruption? Jesus did a powerful miracle in Jairus's interruption. He showed His healing power before He showed His resurrection power. God can heal your affliction. He can do things you can't imagine. He will heal you in ways you don't expect. He'll show you His power to heal, and then He'll resurrect your body from its shadows of death.

This dark time in my recovery wasn't the final chapter of my story. God had a better place that would tend to my needs. I moved on from Fox's in Mechanicsburg back toward my area of residence near Reading. The Laurel Center was less than half an hour from the parsonage I left about four months ago in sudden paralysis.

Settling into My New Home

The front of the Laurel Center building had brick and stone and felt inviting with bushes and trees around it. Two big wheelchair accessible doors welcomed everyone into the building. In the back was a wide, rural-looking yard with a pavilion for meeting outside.

The facility had two sections—a north wing and a south wing. Each wing had three halls. The Laurel Center was home to about 150 residents. I was on the vent hall with two other quadriplegics and anyone who needed a trach; some were on ventilators.

> This seemed like a place of peace.

This became my home for almost four years of my condition. Between the two sections of residential rooms there was the recreation room and office, a couple of dining rooms, an outside patio area for residents to enjoy, a general activities room, industrial kitchen, and administrative offices.

On my hall were two rooms at the end, an observation room overlooking the beautiful outside yard, and a meeting room for people to talk and hold meetings. On another hall was an elevator with access to the basement where the physical therapy and rehab facilities were located. This seemed like a place of peace, a place I might wait on the Lord for my healing. I didn't yet know the new opportunities for ministry God would give me.

My Indescribable Pain

Within a day I was in pain, more than usual. My whole body hurt. I couldn't figure out why. I just wanted to get out of that bed. It dawned on me that this was the first time since the hospital that I was not lying on an air mattress. Once I realized that, it made sense why my body hurt so much.

The mattresses at the Laurel Center were made of memory foam, not nearly as supportive for my condition as the air mattresses. When I asked them if I could get an air mattress, they told me those were for wound care and preventing bedsores. I asked them, "So I have to get a bedsore before I can have the air mattress that prevents them?" There was silence on the other end of that conversation.

Within two days I was begging them to get out of my bed, but there was no wheelchair for me at this facility. They asked the therapy folks if they could find a wheelchair that would work. The closest they could find was a wheelchair operated by the hand joystick. But it was for a guy six feet tall.

The therapy professionals did their best to help it fit me. They put a foot of padding between my feet and the foot pedals in the chair. It got me out of my bed at least for a while. For the most part, the chair was helpful, but it didn't fit my torso either. The sides began cutting into my rib area. Nonetheless, I was thankful for a way to get out of the bed.

I continued to have pain when lying in my bed. They decided to give me a fentanyl patch to relieve my pain. The first night I had the patch I almost threw up at dinner. They lessened the dosage, and I was fine after that. I couldn't understand why they would rather give me a patch every week instead of just getting the air mattress.

I was settling into my new place and making friends. This was certainly a better fit for me than Fox at Mechanicsburg. I was glad to be there, and everyone seemed to know what they were doing and how to take care of me. There were two other quadriplegic people there. I looked forward to finding my niche in this new place.

The Laurel Center Staff

When I arrived at the Laurel Center, I had many new acquaintants to make. Between the nursing staff, respiratory therapist, CNAs, physical therapy staff, recreation staff, and many others, I had to learn many names and faces. The people I remembered the easiest were the CNAs and nurses who daily took care of me.

Respiratory therapists were easy to remember. We had two on my hall during the day and one at night. I got to know two of them well. Many of the staff had a sense of humor, and we got along just fine. The two main respiratory therapists were the only ones I trusted enough to change my trach.

The nurses were a lot of fun. They too had a great sense of humor. One of them proudly wore the alias, "The Poop Queen." Another had the longest red hair I had ever seen. My morning nurse took a lot longer to get to know. She was a bit more rigid than the other nurses, but eventually we got to know one another better.

Most of my CNAs, who cared for me daily—between showers and baths, getting me in and out of my wheelchair, and feeding me—

were very caring. One of my favorite people was a night shift respiratory therapist who had a sharp wit and was extremely sarcastic. We got along really well.

Is Waiting on the Lord Unbiblical?

As mentioned earlier, most of the Gospel healing accounts include the word *immediately*. Most people didn't wait for their healing. Does that mean we should not have to wait on the Lord for our healing? Some people suggest commanding your body to do what it should, and it simply obeys you if you have faith.

You can't speed up your healing. I can command my body to do what I want, but when my brain sends messages to my body, it doesn't respond. I'm not saying something in doubt. This is just my current reality.

The Bible speaks about waiting on the Lord; such waiting has great benefits. This 'waiting' is not what it sounds like. The psalmists talk about waiting as a spiritual act; they understand what we go through as we wait because they went through trouble, too.

They experienced God hiding himself when they were in trouble. God is not at our beck and call. When we want Him to rescue us, we can know that He sees the bigger picture and can use our trial to grow us spiritually. Your affliction does not give you a front row seat to becoming holy. Every Christian experiences God's hiding. St. John of the Cross called this experience "the dark night of the soul."

Ask yourself, *What is God showing me while I wait for Him? How is God guiding me and ministering through me during this time?* People with affliction seek the Lord out of desperation. We have no respite from our pain and suffering. We are keenly aware of our immediate need for the Lord to move in our situation.

What Waiting on the Lord Is Not

We must not get the wrong idea about waiting on the Lord. Don't waste your time in your waiting period. This is a time for deep spiritual reflection and growth. We meet with God in a special way. He molds and shapes us, sometimes changing our ministry approach or enhancing it.

During my waiting time, my call and message have not changed, but the way I deliver them has. It was no different at the Laurel Center. Use your time of affliction for journaling, deeper Bible study, and outreach to your community. This is not a sabbatical. We don't shut ourselves off from the world. Don't wallow in self-pity and doubt. We don't sit around. It's not a time to complain about your affliction, setbacks in your restoration, or to question God why you are going through this.

When I say that these actions waste our time in the waiting period, I want to counter that with the reality that God has a plan to *use* this time. He did not cause your affliction, but as with trials, He wants to grow your faith and character in this time. He wants to minister through you by His Holy Spirit. God will make you fruitful as you wait on Him.

What Does Waiting on the Lord Mean?

What does the Bible say about waiting on the Lord? The Psalms speak much of waiting on the Lord. One song of ascents sung on the way to the temple describes crying out to God, and in waiting for God's answer and help to come, you rely on hope for the Lord (Ps 130).

> Those who wait on the Lord do not just sit around and expect Him to do everything. They patiently anticipate God completing His plans for them and for the world.

Another Psalm describes waiting on the Lord for vindication and gaining courage and strength, knowing that the Lord will respond (Ps 27). In fact, this psalm mentions waiting on the Lord twice (vv. 9, 34). As you wait on the Lord in stillness, delighting in Him, you commit your way to the Lord and live a righteous life. You wait for the Lord to bring justice against the wicked.

Isaiah speaks of fearing the Lord, trusting in Him instead of idols and hoping in the Lord's deliverance (Isa 8:17). He says that those who wait on the Lord renew their strength, run without weariness, and walk without fainting (40:31).

Paul contrasts those who reject living for today and following idols with those who wait for their citizenship in heaven; he notes that we wait for Jesus to transform our bodies to be like His, and for Jesus to subject all things to himself (Phil 3:20).

Waiting on the Lord requires being still before Him, trusting Him to act in your life, and to have patience as He fulfills His will in your life. While you wait on the Lord, you live a righteous life. You trust in the Lord to respond to your request. You gain strength from the Lord. Fear the Lord and worship Him, praising His name as you wait on Him.

Those who wait on the Lord do not just sit around and expect Him to do everything. They patiently anticipate God completing His plans for them and for the world. This means active participation in God's will—not halting your life until God acts.

A Shiny New Wheelchair

I used the loaner wheelchair for about a year before my mom intervened to get me a better one. She found out about a marvelous place called Ricky's Wheels that allows people to take any wheelchair they had as long as they had a prescription from a doctor. You could use one of their wheelchairs until you didn't need it anymore.

Mom told me Ricky's story. His parents own the store. Ricky needed a wheelchair in his affliction. After he passed away, they lent his wheelchair to another person. Their only requirement was to return the wheelchair when it was no longer needed so they could lend it to another person.

When people found out, they donated wheelchairs to the family. They received so many wheelchairs that they started a business where they fix up broken wheelchairs, lend them to people with afflictions, and pay it forward for Ricky. Ricky's parents found their ministry calling.

My mom visited Ricky's Wheels and brought a chair more my size to the Laurel Center. It still had a joystick, which I cannot operate. That one did not suit my needs very well either, so we tried a couple of chairs. Her determination for a useful wheelchair showed the therapy team we were serious.

They found a program that would allow me to get a wheelchair fitted to my body along with the proper mechanism for driving it myself. This was a big step toward my independence. Instead of having to wait for someone to drive me with the joystick I could now move on my own, I would have a wheelchair I could drive myself, just like at MaGee.

Returning to Ministry

About two weeks after I arrived at the Laurel Center, the director of recreation paid me a visit. He asked me if I would hold a service and preach to the community. My face lit up. For the first time since my spinal cord injury, I could do what I was born to do.

I gladly accepted this opportunity. This was as close to full-time pastoral ministry as I had gotten since my injury. From that time, I preached once a week. When the people found out, 35-50 people came to the services. Sometimes people sat in the hallway because there was no room in the recreation room.

There was a wide range of denominations represented in this group. I asked the recreational director if we could serve communion once a month. He got support from several individuals who would help pass out the elements, and we added a communion service. After that, an even greater number of people participated.

During our second communion service, one lady who helped serve communion told me of a resident who could not attend the communion service. I looked at her and said, "Then I will go to him."

We visited his room, and I walked through the communion with him. It touched my heart to see tears running down his face as he partook of each element. He thanked me profusely, and I said that it's only right for believers to share the Lord's Supper together. This became a regular service for anyone who could not attend the communion service.

Ministering at the Laurel Center

Ministering to the elderly for this 30-year-old pastor was not new. I had several elderly saints in my congregation and my church in Shillington. Preparing sermons and services at the Laurel Center was a transition for me because we only had thirty minutes for the whole service. I had to adjust my preaching to fit a new audience. Many people at Laurel were older and had shorter attention spans. When we had communion, there was even less time for the sermon. I had the privilege of preaching to these blessed saints for years.

I used alot of series preaching at Laurel. I began downloading some old-time video hymns to my laptop so they could listen to familiar music before I preached. Some of them told me they didn't want to miss a service. They made it a point to arrive early. I loved preaching to them. Most were quite attentive, and I believe the Lord ministered through me to their need. Even if you have dementia or Alzheimer's, there are some things you don't forget, and one of them is going to church.

One day, a recreation assistant asked me if I could do a memorial service for one of the people who passed away. I didn't know the person, but I gathered information about the deceased from an obituary and basic information from the recreation assistant. The deceased person was someone who had gone to the services I preached at Laurel.

I prepared a short memorial service, which about twenty people attended. After I did my part, I asked if anyone wanted to share something about the deceased. After the memorial service, the recreation assistant thanked me profusely. I was glad to do the memorial service.

Another time, the recreational director approached me with another opportunity. He told me about a man who often attended our church services who was about to pass away. He wondered if I would go to the man's room and spend time with him and his family.

This was a new experience for me. I had never been involved in hospice care. I just tried to be there for them, going to his room and ministering to him and his family. They asked me about what the Bible says about death. I shared Psalm 116:15, "Precious to the Lord is the death of His saints," and other Scriptures.

They felt relieved and grateful for my ministry. My ministerial presence gave them peace, and they appreciated my service. The man passed away that night. Thankfully, he was ready to meet Jesus. There's nothing like the moment when Jesus's friends pass from this life to the next.

These new experiences at Laurel gave me different facets of ministry than I experienced at my church in Shillington. Jesus was with me as I stepped outside my comfort zone into the waters of these ministry opportunities. Jesus made up the difference between my abilities and experiences and my obedience to do whatever He put in front of me. The Holy Spirit was with me, and I knew I wasn't ministering in my own strength.

Don't Do It on Your Own

I had to rely on Jesus every step of this new ministry experience at Laurel. We must not try to fulfill God's promise merely with our own resources. God spoke to Abraham and promised to give him a son (Gen 15:4-6). He and Sarah waited twenty-five years to see God's fulfillment of this promise, but they became impatient. Sarah suggested to Abraham that he have a son by Hagar, her servant (16:2), but after Hagar conceived and had her son, Ishmael, Sarah became jealous of Hagar. Abraham and Sarah thought they could fulfill God's promise with Ishmael, but that was not God's plan. All it did was cause strife that still exists between Arabs and Jews today.

If only Abraham and Sarah had waited on the Lord to do the impossible to fulfill His promise, it would have saved them from strife. God will heal your affliction. Even if it looks impossible, believe that nothing is impossible with God (Luke 1:37). Temptations will come for you to do it with your resources or seek healing from other ways, but don't give in to those temptations.

What's My Ministry?

Full-time ministry is not everyone's call. Every Christian has some call from God to minister, but one believer's ministry will look different from another's. How do you know what your ministry is? Think about your ministry field. What's your corner of the world where God has planted you? What are the people like? What do they need spiritually?

> Every Christian has some call from God to minister.

Maybe you can offer practical helps like mowing the grass or home repair work. Perhaps they need a friend or have questions about your faith. Be a faithful friend and neighbor. Care for any of the needs in your community. God may use you at your job. Be open to every opportunity to serve others. That's what the best ministries look like.

Ask the Lord how He wants to minister through you. Go through a spiritual gifts assessment and training. Know your gifts and how the Holy Spirit wants to minister through you. Find resources to equip yourself to serve. Be open to opportunities to minister to others. Share your faith in open door opportunities. Be present, willing to serve, and faithful to your community.

Starting the Quad Club

I went outside to the back patio at Laurel as much as one of the staff could take me out. I enjoyed talking to staff and being outside. It was relaxing to take in the scenery. One respiratory therapist took me outside regularly. I began to realize that the other quadriplegics didn't get out of their rooms. It's good for quadriplegics to interact with others. So, I convinced them to come outside and hang out. We enjoyed one another's company. We called our time together "The Quad Club." We got together regularly, though not planned. We talked about sports, music, politics, and current events. We told stories about our experiences as quadriplegics.

One quadriplegic friend had lived at the Laurel Center since he was sixteen. He told us stories about his relationships with the staff and residents. My other quadriplegic friend received his spinal cord injury while playing wide receiver in arena football. By day he worked at Olive Garden, but by night he played football. It was the love of his life, and he enjoyed talking about football. We liked different teams. Where else would you get Cowboys, Giants, and Steelers fans together?

We started getting together inside for special occasions. When we all got our wheelchairs, we had a pizza party. The recreation assistant set everything up. She got a projector and a giant sheet to play a movie. My mom brought in pizza and hung out with us. We had a great time.

One of my friends became a believer in Jesus. Unfortunately, I am the only one still living. After I left, I found out that my football friend had passed away. About a year later, my other friend died. God had put us together to enrich one another's lives.

While You Wait...

While we wait on the Lord, we have hope that God will finish our healing. He ministers to your spirit as you wait on Him. Don't let your faith become stagnant as you wait. Keep your hope in His promises alive. God works in the background of your life as you work for Him.

Live the Christian life and be an example of godly living. Bless and encourage others. Be persistent in your prayers. Grow in your ministry to others. Be faithful and open to opportunities to serve others.

The enemy doesn't know how to react to Job-like faith.

Trust God to fulfill His promises. He has never failed. You know beyond a shadow of a doubt that God will come through for you. Live as though you are already healed. Speak in faith about God and your healing. Be active in good deeds. Be patient for the Lord to answer your prayer. Focus on Jesus and act according to His Word. Do what you know is the Lord's will. Don't doubt or fear.

After preaching, I would pray for others with afflictions. I didn't consciously realize that I was confounding the enemy by praying for others with afflictions. It doesn't make sense in the natural, but it is a powerful spiritual act. No matter what you are going through, pray for others with afflictions. God may use you to heal them, and them to heal you. The more we show our faith, pray for others with similar conditions, and act out our faith as though our healing has already happened, the more we confuse the enemy. He doesn't know how to react to Job-like faith.

You are still alive. Don't act as though you are dead. Find out what He wants you to do, and do it with your whole being. Thank God for improvements to your condition. I learned to thank God for pain. Most quadriplegics cannot feel anything. When my nerves give me pain, I thank God I can feel something. I am training my brain to realize my healing is coming.

What can you learn from God in your experience? God does not cause affliction, but He can guide us and teach us about His nature as we grow in our relationship with Him. Don't dwell on the past that took place before your affliction. Learn from the Israelites in the wilderness who wanted to return to Egypt, the house of slavery. God has greater things for you ahead.

> You are still alive. Don't act as though you are dead.

I have more time now than I ever had to study God's Word, to pray and seek the Lord, to minister to people and churches with my ability to build websites, to do intercessory prayer, to write in my blog and books, and to teach the Word. How can God minister through you in your waiting period?

Activities at the Laurel Center

The Laurel Center had many activities for the residents. If I got bored in my room, I would head to the activities room and see what was happening. They did everything from playing bocce ball with larger balls to having a movie day. Of course, the movies and TV shows the residents watched were "oldies but goodies." I got quite the education from movies and TV shows that I had not even known existed.

I especially enjoyed card games, going outside on the patio, and mouth painting. That's right. I had first tried it when I was at MaGee. The aid there set me up with a giant painting easel that my chair could fit under, which she made in her own time and brought for me to use. She prepared the paints and colors I wanted and placed either a paintbrush or a special stick that held the paintbrushes and writing utensils in my mouth.

It takes practice to put things where you want them on the canvas or a piece of paper. So I told the activities director at Laurel about this form of recreation. He was willing to try anything I thought I could do. I became adept at handling paintbrushes with the special device I could fit in my mouth. Later, I began painting without the device, which made my strokes less accurate. Because I don't have the vision, putting the stick on this extra device was even harder for me. You can check out some of my mouth paintings in my Facebook images at facebook.com/jonathan.srock.

The Benefits of Waiting on God

We have much to learn during this time of waiting on the Lord. I used to be able to do everything for myself. I didn't have to rely on others. But my paralysis is teaching me that I'm not in control, to lean on the kindness and help of others, and to keep my anger in check.

The Lord teaches us patience as we wait. When we feel desperate for Him to act, we have no recourse but to wait. We learn to depend on God for our every need. We cannot do it for ourselves. Our faith and trust in God grow as we wait. We rely on Him for our provision. God proves His faithfulness to us.

When we have a need we can fulfill with our resources, we leap forward without looking to God or listening to His voice. We trust in our provision. We see our abundance as God's blessing. It's not that we don't seek God, but we don't rely on Him as much as we need Him to act on our behalf. We learn by experience these truths about God.

Waiting on the Lord keeps us from acting before we know God's will in each matter. We benefit from His wisdom. He saves us the pains and stresses we put on ourselves when we don't seek Him first. Waiting on the Lord gives us pause in an overly busy world. Worldly values teach us to get what we can for ourselves, to be impatient, to be ambitious, and to envy and covet. We grasp for possessions and power.

Jacob deceived others to get what he could for himself. One night, after separating his camp into two to protect at least part of his wealth, before he met his brother, Jacob ran into the Angel of the Lord (Gen 32:22-32). He wrestled with the angel, asking His name to control him, and refusing to let the angel go without blessing him.

But Jacob's way of manipulating people would not work with the angel. He had to surrender and give the angel his name, which means deceiver or heel grabber. He came face-to-face with the truth about himself. His freedom came in surrendering to the truth about who he really was and how he deceived others. When we wait on the Lord, we learn about ourselves. We starve our selfish desires and will. We seek the Lord instead of worldly ways. Waiting on the Lord renews our God given priorities.

Keep Hope Alive

Most of all, Jesus gives you inklings of your healing through His faithfulness and provision. He shows you who He is as you wait on

Him. He keeps sure hope alive. We learn to trust in Him all over again. We seek His face out of desperation, and He gives us more than we could have imagined.

Wait on the Lord; He renews your strength (Isa 40: 31). He guides you through the storms of life. He shows himself faithful to you. He rekindles your relationship and trust in Him. He proves His love for you. You learn to leave the hustle and bustle of the rat race behind. You find Jesus as your only treasure.

Waiting on the Lord becomes your desire instead of the things of this world. You find God amid pain and loss. In losing everything you held dear you find the One you hold even dearer. He satisfies every need you have. He lavishes His love and grace upon you. Like Paul, we leave what is behind and press on toward God and His upward call for us (Phil 3:13-14). Let us press into the presence of God and seek Him, find Him, and rest in His provision for us in the middle space between the promise and its fulfillment. Here we find our peace. Jesus is all we need.

Prepare for War

Waiting on the Lord will be your Waterloo if you don't follow the steps in this chapter. Take this time for active ministry in your life. This is no time to sit on the sidelines. Get in the game!

What are your ministry gifts from the Holy Spirit? How can you serve the people around you? Your ministry may change. Embrace new ministry opportunities. Watch the Holy Spirit prepare you for these new adventures.

Spend your time on spiritual growth. Practice the spiritual disciplines. Seek the Lord for your healing. Serve your community faithfully.

Chapter 6
Demolish Your Doubt

"Truly I say to you, whoever says to this mountain, 'Be lifted up and thrown into the sea,' and does not hesitate in his heart, but believes that what he is saying is happening, it will happen for him." (Mark 11:23)

"But he must ask in faith without doubt, because the doubter is like a wave of the sea, driven and blown by the wind." (James 1:6)

I talk a good game about faith and hope in the dark times, but I have fought hard against doubt, fear, and feelings that God has left me to wallow in pity and ask the hard question, "Why me?" Like Job, I wonder why I have to go through this. Where is God in our suffering?

It is natural for a person facing a slew of afflictions to question whether everything makes sense and to wonder about God's abandonment and the point of suffering if you can't just make it all go away. If you are a person of faith and don't ask these questions, you have lost your grip on reality.

Each of us who suffers an affliction, especially a terminal or ongoing one that doctors don't have answers for, needs to deal with these questions that seemed so easy to answer before our affliction.

When you live through the questions of suffering, God's existence and why He lets you go through these things are no longer existential or ethereal discussions. They apply to where you live. You are not an outside observer looking in on the problem of pain and sickness. You are living them, and the answer to these questions weighs heavily upon you.

So, what do we do as we walk through our suffering and have these questions? How do we take a stand in faith and hope when we receive no hope from the doctors? This is the hardest trial of them all. It goes beyond our sickness to the questions we have of God during these valleys. But we are not alone. We have a great cloud of witnesses—strong saints who have forged the path of suffering before us. We turn to questions of doubt, fear, and anxiety.

The Years of Setbacks

While I was at the Laurel Center, I experienced setbacks among my positive steps forward. I was hospitalized twice, had a couple of infections very dangerous to my health, and fought harder than before to maintain hope in God's promises and Word. But God proved himself over and over to me.

> Don't think that every negative experience you have is the devil coming after you.

My years of setbacks to my condition, challenges to my health, and intense emotion to navigate challenged the positive changes of ministry, faith, and hope. These were years of spiritual and physical battles. You are not less of a Christian if you face adversity. You are not spiritually scrawny, a royal screwup, or being punished. Break the chains of those lies of the enemy. If he comes after you, you're doing something right. You have become a threat to him. But don't think that every negative experience you have is the devil coming after you. We all make mistakes and don't use godly wisdom.

One way you know the devil is coming after you is when you have spiritual influence. You are ministering in the Spirit's power, seeing God work through you, and building up spiritual capital. Lives are changing because of God's ministry through you.

There were many good things that happened at the Laurel Center. I thank God that He was with me through these battles and helped me navigate these rough times. I experienced the most pain and challenges to my faith there as much as I enjoyed a renewed openness to ministry. As I look back on those years now, I can see how God encouraged me despite these setbacks.

The pain and suffering I went through, and sometimes still suffer, surprised me. I had infections and minor setbacks I could never have imagined. I'm sharing my experiences to encourage you. In the same way, your struggles and the way you handle them can inspire someone to press on in their faith.

The lessons you learn and the relationship you build with God in your affliction can help others. What you deal with, and what you get out of it, are lessons you may not learn except in living your experience and sharing the wisdom, guidance, and relationship you would not have had but for that very experience and affliction.

As you read about my experiences, think about your suffering and pain through the years. Have setbacks discouraged your faith and brought doubt into your relationship with Jesus? How do you answer the questions about where God is in your suffering?

It's hard not to take these scholarly arguments about pain and suffering and why God allows it to happen to us and talk about them as you experience them. You didn't learn about this in the ivory towers of theology. You are walking through the mire of trust versus doubt and fear versus courage. Your experiences give you a diploma that rivals those of scholars.

Your Blessings and Reminders

I saw the wheelchair I received at the Laurel Center in two ways. It was a blessing from God, but it was also a reminder of my paralysis during this season of my life. The dark places of doubt and questioning God are not the only thing you encounter in your valley. God's blessings still come upon you.

God comforts you with overflowing mercies that pour out from you onto others (2 Cor 1:3-5). God confronts you when you get comfortable with your affliction. He goes to battle against your doubts, fears, and anxieties. He doesn't let them torment you.

But you must drag them out of your closet, out of the dark, and let His light shine on them. When you slay them, they can come back to torment you again. You must learn how to keep bringing them before Jesus. You have a gift for ministry to others in similar situations because of your experiences. God can use your affliction to let blessing flow through you to others.

Our good God does great things through us despite our afflictions. God does not cause your affliction, but He doesn't stop His predestined program to conform you to the image of Christ (Rom 8:29), change your perspective, and deepen His relationship with you either.

God works in ways we cannot understand. His ways are higher than our ways (Isa 55:9). He gives us a peace that passes our understanding (Phil 4:7). He gives us joy, even if only in small pockets and turns our mourning into dancing (Ps. 30:11). He never leaves us (Heb 13:5). Jesus's presence is there in the worst of times.

If you can't feel His presence in this time, believe He is there. He is working His plan of growth, strength, and holiness in you. God never leaves or forsakes you (Heb 13:5). As a seasoned saint, don't allow the devil to convince you that God is not walking with you.

Stand on God's Word and promises—and put the devil in his place.

Shingles, Really?

One morning, I woke up to a searing pain on my face. It felt like someone had lit a match and rubbed it across the left side of my face and eye. I blew on a straw to ring my call bell. One of the CNAs came to my room and took one look at my face.

"You look worried," I observed.

"I'll be right back," she said. And with that, she left the room.

She returned with a couple of nurses. They examined my face. "That looks like shingles," one nurse said.

I vaguely remembered what shingles was. I thought it was something that happened to old people.

The pain was getting worse. They informed me that it had somehow developed right over my left eye. I had wondered why it hurt so much there, and now I knew! What I didn't know was how *much* pain shingles causes.

The pain continued to get worse. I thought pain was bad, but this was much worse. I couldn't concentrate. Just when I thought I was maxed out on pain, it got worse. I cried myself to sleep, but there was no sleep.

There was no running from this disease, no eye of the storm, no way to distract myself from it. At least with pain I could distract myself by watching something on TV or on my computer. But this pain kept me even from those things.

My mom came to visit me while I had shingles. She took a picture so I could see the damage. I looked like some alien from *Star Trek*. I had brown spots all over that part of my face and eye. Why would they show up right there? Apparently, shingles on your face and eyes is more painful than other places on your body. *Why me?*

I don't remember how long I had shingles. I only remember crying myself to sleep, except that I couldn't sleep. I cried until there were no more tears. There was no relief. It's the worst pain I have ever experienced.

Somehow the Lord healed me of shingles. You would never be able to tell today that I had this experience. They left no scars or marks on my face. I hope never to experience that high of a level of pain again.

Why Me?

Anyone who suffers an affliction like paralysis, a life-changing affliction, shingles, constant infections, and fiery nerve pain should ask, "Why me?" Quadriplegic paralysis is a lifelong injury. You don't reverse this condition scientifically or naturally. You start to wonder what you did to deserve this—but you don't deserve it. It's a spiritual and physical battle.

My first thoughts after my paralysis and my realization of how my life would change weren't exactly this question. I had served God faithfully. I had enjoyed ministry. But it seemed that was all being taken away from me. Job asked the same question.

God may never tell us why the enemy targets us. He may not give you the details of why you suffer your affliction.
But you can remain faithful.

You would be crazy *not* to ask. Sometimes God answers you. Other times, like in Job's case, God may never tell you why you suffer. When I realized in the hospital that I could not even speak, this was my first question. Throughout the years of my paralysis, I still wonder why, especially when my pain levels shoot up.

I searched my mind to see if I did something wrong or was unhealthy in any way to cause this. I could think of nothing. I asked God why this happened to me. I was already dealing with legal blindness since birth. Now I could not move my limbs on my body or regulate my breathing or body temperature. I couldn't minister in full-time ministry as a pastor anymore.

I got the impression that like Job I faced the rage of the enemy. After thinking about Job and knowing that God does not bring affliction on His children, I had no other conclusion than that the devil was angry with what I was preaching and teaching. I didn't think I had much spiritual sway considering my congregation was small, but something I was doing got his attention. I had found myself on his radar, and he wasn't playing fair.

The devil will do whatever he can to keep you from fulfilling the call given to you by God. He may not be behind your affliction, but if he is, he will fight you tooth and nail for every inch of your recovery. He'll play mind games and make you question God instead of him.

Job didn't know the devil existed, but we know from the first couple of chapters in Job that Satan targeted Job because he was faithful to God and would not break under the pressure of his affliction. God chose him because he was faithful to Him.

God may never tell us why the enemy targets us. He may not give you the details of why you suffer your affliction. But you can remain faithful. You can ask questions. You can question God and your existence like Job did, but God may not answer you. All you can do is remain faithful to the Lord.

My First Panic Attack

Some things take longer to process than others. Once I arrived at the Laurel Center, I had a terrible panic attack. I was lying in my bed, and the implications of my paralysis hit me. My paralysis meant I was trapped in my body, a prisoner from movement and feeling. I panicked for the first time.

I rang my call bell, and when the CNA arrived at my bedside I was still panicking. I tried to move my limbs and was saying, "I've got to get out of here. I've got to get out of here." She thought I was talking about leaving the Laurel Center. I was talking about my body.

I felt trapped and wanted to move on my own. I was used to doing things for myself, independently, but now I was stuck and could not control my body. I didn't know whether I could live like this. I just wanted out. I wanted things to go back to the way they used to be—to what the devil had stolen from me.

These thoughts flooded over me. I had always preached about healing, but now I was living the reality of paralysis. I didn't think I could cope with my situation. For the first time in my life, this was one giant I could not overcome. The mountain of my problem became bigger than my God.

I felt like everything was being taken away from me. I didn't realize who I was without the ministry.

As an ordained minister, I believed with my head that God is always bigger than my problems. But in my heart, I saw an impossible, impassable mountain. How would I come back from paralysis? I can't pastor a church and promise them I will be there for every event, let alone every service and Bible study. How could I minister in a church?

I had to give up my church because of paralysis. We didn't know how long it would take me to pastor the church again. The longer this process lasted, the more we realized I wasn't going to be ready to pastor the church. I felt like everything was being taken away from me. I didn't realize who I was without the ministry.

All of this compounded upon my heart, and the cage of not being able to move, the reality of paralysis in my life and ministry caused a breaking point in me. It was all I could do to keep my sanity. I just wanted everything to go back to the way it was before my paralysis. I was losing it. I wanted out of my prison, and I didn't know how. I could do nothing to change my circumstance. Only God could do that.

This CNA was finally able to calm me down. I had never experienced such a moment of hopelessness, of sudden reaction to my circumstances before. I don't know what came over me. Looking back on that experience, I wonder what unbelievers, who have no one to turn to, do with the kind of hopelessness that I felt.

It's OK to Cry and Panic

It's only human to react to our circumstances. It's not wrong, and you can't avoid it. When faced with extreme circumstances like our afflictions, we can't help but react—usually negatively. But we must not stay in that space. Faith must take hold in the face of perplexing situations.

Our immediate reaction is to cry out to God. We ask Him to change everything immediately. If He doesn't, we question our faith, question God, and question our understanding of ourselves and our world. We see the walls closing in on us. *How could this happen to me?*

You would either be a psychological marvel or accused of not living in reality if you didn't react to your suffering. You need to recognize your circumstances before you can see God move in powerful ways in your life. Your initial reaction is healthy psychologically. But if you stay in that space and keep having that reaction, you will never experience spiritual healing.

After we acknowledge our affliction, we must turn to the Lord for answers and for His power to work in our situation. Jesus may not answer your questions, but He is with you. His presence is more than enough. Jesus replaces your panic with a peace that passes understanding (Phil 4:7).

When overwhelming circumstances threaten to crush your spirit, turn to the Holy Spirit. He gives you God's power and strength to overcome it. You don't do this on your own. You need Him to give you the strength to face your affliction with His power instead of your own.

Instead of panicking, your new trial is to learn to turn to Jesus and trust Him instead of trusting in your resources or allowing your affliction to become bigger than your trust in God.

A Series of Infections

I don't remember why, but for a time I was having migraines when I was laying in my bed. They could have been caused by my pillow, my mattress being too hard, or some other reason. The migraines were terrible, producing another terrible pain. The light in the room was making me feel nauseous, so I asked for the lights and TV to be turned off. The caregivers could not close the blinds. Instead of dealing with the issues that could help me feel better, though, they gave me another medicine.

I had a couple of UTIs, one which left me in a septic state. It was a very dangerous infection. I could have died from being septic. They wanted to give me an IV for antibiotics. I really hate needles, so I was against the idea, not realizing how dangerous it was. I finally agreed at the urging of my parents. I was too out of it to even realize they put one in. That was a relief for me. The antibiotics brought the septic status under control.

I was still getting an allergic reaction to something I was taking, which was causing a nasty rash. They couldn't figure out what it was. To stop my allergic reaction of my skin turning red, they gave me steroids. But unfortunately, this just made the rash on my skin worse. I looked like a lobster. They got so worried that they sent me to Lehigh Valley Hospital. This was around June or July of 2016.

While in the hospital to get a biopsy, I began seeing things. This was the first time I had ever experienced anything like this. At one point, I saw numbers and letters crawling on the walls like a startup routine on a giant computer monitor. I couldn't understand why no one could see it. They must have thought I was crazy.

Along with the letters on the wall, I had terrible nightmares. I woke up in the middle of the night several times that first week, freaking out about what I saw. It felt like I was crawling up and down the walls. It took a while for the nurses to calm me down. When I woke up from the nightmares, I saw people standing in my room who weren't really there. I realized that this was a demonic attack. So I battled in prayer pleading the blood of Jesus over myself.

We soon discovered that one of the meds they put me on at the hospital that really threw me for a loop was the culprit, so they changed my medication to something that didn't cause delusions. When they changed my medicine, everything returned to normal. This does not diminish the spiritual attack against me. The people in my room disappeared, and I had no more terrible nightmares. I almost thought I was going crazy. My doctor reduced the medicines I took, streamlining them so they did not counteract each other.

Comatose

In addition to the hospitalization for the rash in the summer of 2016, I was admitted to Lehigh Valley Hospital again in September for coma-like symptoms.

I opened my eyes one Friday morning to see several concerned respiratory therapist, nurses, and CNAs. My respiratory therapist friend, Dave, came over to me. He was talking about taking me to the hospital because I was unresponsive. I drifted off before I heard anything else.

A few days later, on the morning of Friday, September 9, the nurses at the nursing home could not wake me. This had become a regular occurrence. I remembered several instances waking up and being asked if I knew where I was and who these people were at the nursing home. So, they sent me to the hospital to find out what was making it so hard to wake me.

I had been taking Botox injections in my arms to help them stay loose for physical therapy. But because of my recent migraines we had tried Botox injections in my neck. Some of the side effects of Botox injections are especially severe, including slurring your words, falling asleep randomly, and trouble chewing and swallowing. I had not put all this together over the last couple of months.

I must have woken up while I was there because I remember the room I was in. I didn't know where I was other than in a hospital. I could not have been awake for long. Things got very strange. I could hear people talking around me and could even visualize them, but I noticed I could "rewind" and "fast-forward" their visits with me. When family visited, I could move back and forward in time with their visits.

I thought it was my imagination. I didn't realize that I never talked to the nurses or my family. But that was only the first dream I was trapped in. I next found myself in what I perceived to be a play. When I looked down at my body, it was a skeleton.

As in real life, I played a preacher, but I was standing on the street declaring the gospel to passersby. The devil would come to me and torment me: "You don't really believe that nonsense. When you die, you will be with me."

I stood on the Word and told the devil to get lost. But he would continue to heckle me on the street. I declared my faith in Jesus and found myself relaxing in my room after the play, but then I would be called again to play my part.

This continued for some time. I did not know the passage of days and nights, but I eventually found myself in a third dream. It was very cold. It felt like the ice storms I endured in Springfield, Missouri when I was going to school there. It was bone chilling cold.

When I looked down at my body this time, the bones were fragmented and apart from one another. I discovered I was lying in a coffin. As with my paralysis, I could not move to get anyone's attention. I could hear family and friends eulogizing me. I realized I was attending my own funeral.

I was yelling and trying to get everyone's attention. I was trying to tell them I was not dead, but it got colder and colder. I heard the doctor talking to my mom, telling her there was no brain activity and that she should consider the possibility of turning off the machines and letting me go.

"I'm alive! Your machines and tests are wrong! Why won't anyone listen to me?"

The devil came a final time and said, "You will soon be mine. Jesus can't save you now."

"I know Jesus lives. He has promised me a place with Him forever. You are the father of lies and I stand in the truth of Jesus's promise to me. Go away."

The devil left. I kept seeing a light in my eyes, as if my eyelids were shut. I could hear voices: "Jonathan, move your eyes from side to side. Smile." I responded by moving my eyes and smiling. "No response." I couldn't understand why they didn't see me respond.

They came again and again with the same tests. I repeatedly followed their instructions to hear them say, "No response." I was becoming perturbed and angry. I was sure these nurses and doctors didn't know what they were doing. Where did they get their medical degrees?

I noticed my body changing. After some time, my skeleton was being knitted together, and my body was whole again. I saw muscles and skin forming over them. Again, the doctors came shining that bright light in my eyes. It was clearer than before. Here came the same tests. "Jonathan, move your eyes and smile."

I rolled my eyes and smiled.

"He's responding! He's responding! Jonathan, we thought we had lost you for sure."

I realized I hadn't been responsive for eight days. They told me I was in a coma for eight days. My dreams, the interaction with my family members, hearing the doctor speaking to my mom—everything I heard—was incorporated into that comatose state.

Over the next couple of days, it became clear what had happened to me. All along the way my faith was challenged, but I remained steadfast in Jesus.

I had endured an eight-day coma. After my coma, I was on kidney dialysis for about four weeks. Because I required the kidney dialysis I was sent to the Holy Spirit Hospital for these treatments for that 4-6 weeks. Finally, back at the Laurel Center, they assigned me a speech therapist and put me on a puréed diet around the Holidays. My parents came and brought a machine to puree our Holiday dinner food from home. This persisted until 2 weeks before I left there to come home.

Stand on God's Word and His Promises

In my comatose dreams, my faith had been tested, but I testified to the truth of God's Word and His promises. It was no mistake that I played the part of a preacher on the streets proclaiming God's Word. I vehemently opposed Satan when he tried to convince me that God was lying. I refused to give him an inch. The devil is a liar. We must be convinced that he lies and that the Spirit of truth has shown us the true reality of ourselves and our afflictions. I fought hard against the idea that heaven didn't exist. You must be convinced of the truths of the Bible and stand fast against opposing views. This is how we fight and win our battles.

> My dreams in my coma were a battle for my soul between God and the devil.

I stood firm in my convictions about God and His Word. The devil came against me over and over. At one point, I wavered. But then I stood firm again and never looked back. I believe my dreams in my coma were a battle for my soul between God and the devil. I can only imagine what other comatose patients go through.

My coma could have resulted in my death if I hadn't resisted the devil. It was a turning point for me. We must take the devil's attacks seriously. He will do everything in his power to sway us away from Jesus. With every attack, we must stand on God's Word and His promises. He saves our lives with His truth. You must be certain and knowledgeable about God's Word to combat the devil's advances.

Don't Give the Devil a Foothold

I fought the devil at every turn in my coma. We must realize the battle between faith and doubt. We must fight for victory over anything that comes against God's promises. Fighting for faith is spiritual warfare. As Paul said four times when he talked about the armor of God, you must stand firm (Eph 6:11, 13-14).

Most spiritual warfare happens through prayer, but your resolve must beat the devil through faith. We hold on to God's promises more than anything. Don't let anything sway you. Don't listen to anyone who tells you it's impossible.

Doubt is a cancer that grows inside of us. Just as we put our old fleshly desires in their place, we must place our spiritual capitol in hope and faith. Spend more time in the Word than in the world. Focus on Jesus. Memorize, meditate, and repeat God's promises of healing to you. Study the miracles of the Bible.

All these actions serve as spiritual warfare against doubt and the enemy of your soul. If you give the devil an inch, he will take a mile. Focusing on God's promises for your healing gives you the edge to see your miracle happen. In the Gospels, Jesus required two things for a miracle. First, He used *His power* to heal. Second, He required *faith* expressed in actions and words.

The actions of studying healing, professing your belief that God will heal you of your affliction, speaking from faith, and acting on your healing show your faith. God provides His power to finish the work of healing.

The Enemies of Faith

Faith has enemies. These enemies try to hold you in their grip, but you must resist them. I have fought fear, doubt, worry, and anxiety. Each of these is an enemy of faith. Doubt contradicts faith. It places just a seed of its dangerous and contagious pathogen into your system. Little by little, doubt gets a hold of you, sinking its fingers into your faith. It uses outside circumstances to convince you of the lies of the enemy.

Fear results when you have accepted the lies of doubt. If God is not for you, if His promises will not be fulfilled for you, these fears replace faith. Not all fear melts your faith. Fear is natural and helpful when life-threatening situations present themselves to us. If you are afraid of snakes, you have good reason. One snakebite from the most poisonous snakes will kill you in a matter of seconds.

That's not the fear that destroys faith. It's the fear that comes when we stop believing in God's promises and His Word. You will allow the lies of the enemy to grip your soul. You've lost the spiritual battle. All you have left is fear, worry, and anxiety—the natural results of letting doubts creep in.

We must be careful in how we speak – not from worry, fear, or anxiety. Because of my first trach change, I have had anxiety every month when the nurses change it. I try to play word games when my parents call me on the carpet. I quickly change the word "worry" to "concern." The way I use this word doesn't change my emotions and actions. It's an excuse I used to keep worrying.

I explain that they can't understand it without experiencing it. Even when I close my eyes, I can still see that first trach change. But they don't have to experience what I experience to speak words of faith into my life. I must choose to trust in God's truth.

The explanation that my trach changes go much better now doesn't change my mind. The mind can become a powerful adversary to our faith if we allow it. I can command my thoughts to align with the truth of Scripture, but my mind fights the truth. Jesus gives us the ability to control our thoughts, and take them captive (2 Cor 10:5). Don't choose anxiety and worry over faith.

Faith tells us that God sees us and is there with us, but in contrast, worry comes as doubt's evil twin brother. We worry and have anxiety because doubt has overtaken us. We don't see the reality of God's Word. Many of our negative emotional states—from anxiety to depression—happen because we have lost faith.

I have fought the battle against fear and worry more through my paralysis than at any other time in my life. As I've mentioned, my biggest fear was trach changes, but I have recently found a weapon that slays my fears and brings me peace. I contact my team of prayer warriors to intercede for me on the days I have trach changes. They intercede for me, and I have not dwelt on my trach changes anymore.

My other big fear happened at the Hershey Medical Center when I questioned the Lord if I would ever preach and minister for Him again. So much of me had gone into ministry that I couldn't see myself without it. God had called me to preach, and without a voice and paralysis in those early days, I doubted His call on my life. God had to teach me that I am more than a preacher and teacher. I am His child.

> God confirmed that He has me
> in the palm of His hand.

Once I valued being God's child and called God my Father, I understood my identity in Jesus aside from His call. In that time, God restored ministry to me. He showed me the fear I had of losing my identity and ministry but confirmed that He has me in the palm of His hand. I still must place my faith in God's plan. I am a work in progress. I haven't reached my destiny yet. The Holy Spirit is a comforting Friend when I have moments of fear or anxiety.

"I Believe. Help My Unbelief."

Jesus dealt with doubt and unbelief in His ministry (Matt 9:20-24). Once, His disciples could not cast out a demon that had attacked a boy. The dramatic attacks of the demon from childhood seemed impossible to remedy. Since the disciples could not cast it out, they brought the boy to Jesus.

The father explained his condition and then said, "If you can do anything, have compassion on us and help us" (Matt 9:22). Jesus seized upon, "If you can." He saw the doubt in the father. Jesus simply said, "All things are possible for those who believe." Doubt does not bring miraculous power for healing.

We must have faith that God can do the impossible. Do you have an impossible affliction that doctors have said they can do nothing about for you? This father sounds desperate when he cries out, "I believe. Help my unbelief" (Matt 9:24). He just wanted his boy to be normal.

> His Spirit gently blows over the little embers of our faith until they glow more and more and catch fire for our healing.

We can gain courage from this father's statement. When the disciples realized the power of faith, they asked Jesus to increase their faith (Mark 9:24; Luke 17:5). In our moments of doubt, we can cry out with the same prayer: "I believe. Help my unbelief." Jesus can increase our faith. His Spirit gently blows over the little embers of our faith until they glow more and more and catch fire for our healing.

How to Talk about Your Affliction

There is a theology of how we use our words and thoughts. When the angel Gabriel appeared to Zechariah and told him that Elizabeth, his wife, would be pregnant and bear them a son, Zechariah spoke in disbelief, and so the angel took his voice until John the Baptist was born.

We must be careful what we speak over ourselves and others. Yet we cannot ignore our affliction and act as though it's not happening to us. When we speak our reality, we follow it with faith. While we must be careful with what we say, acknowledging our reality opens the door for Jesus to do miraculous healing in our bodies.

> When we speak our reality, we follow it with faith.

When you go to the altar for prayer for your affliction, you are following the scriptural command in James through the Holy Spirit as you seek healing. The way you talk about your affliction either shows faith or doubt. God gave us powerful words to speak. They can change our situation.

If you speak without faith, you will speak judgment on yourself. But when you cry out to God and talk about your affliction, you don't speak your affliction on yourself. There's no better place to be or people to talk to than the elders of your church (Jas 5: 14-16).

Since my paralysis, no one looks at me in my wheelchair and thinks everything is okay. I can't hide my fortune. If I don't ask for prayer, I accept my condition. When I ask for prayer, describe my condition, and speak words of faith, I reject my affliction as I wait for Jesus to heal me.

Can I Doubt or Be Afraid?

Job is our example of how to remain faithful to God and still have doubts and fears. He speaks in faith, and the Bible says he did not sin against God (Job 1:22; 2:10). We can have faith in God to fulfill His healing promises and still have doubts and fear in our circumstances. We must not allow doubt or fear to take us captive, though. We must stand on God's Word and hold His promises close to us. When you have doubts or feel fear, rebuke them. Turn them over to God and experience His freedom. Let your faith vanquish doubt and fear.

Do not be afraid to share your doubt and fear with a mentor. Your mentor must be a seasoned believer who understands that the Bible does not rebuke us for doubt and fear. Job is one example of how the Bible openly deals with these enemies of the faith. Let the light of God's truth expose and defeat your fears and doubts.

Are My Anxieties Unbelief?

No. Some of the greatest saints in the Bible experienced depression and anxiety, but they turned to God. Those who didn't bring such problems to God fell away from Him. Just because you experience worry, anxiety, anger, fear, and doubt does not make you an unbeliever. It makes you human.

God is bigger than your problems. He has broad shoulders and can handle the challenges you face and the questions you raise. Like Job, you can ask without doubting. It's God's prerogative to answer your questions.

He can handle your moments of anger, anguish, and panic. He can handle your doubts and fears. Don't hide fear, doubt, and anxiety. Run to Jesus, and let the emotions of the moment—the fear and doubt, as well as your setbacks—flow. Jesus will bring you back to an even stronger faith than you had before your affliction.

Have Courage to Crush Your Enemies

People have pointed out that bravery is addressing fear head on. When you feel fear in a crisis, with courage you can defeat it. Spiritual courage works the same way. Crush the enemies of doubt, fear, and anxiety by facing them, taking them to Jesus, and receiving His peace and strength. Courage calls you to bring these enemies into the light and to let Jesus minister to you. Like sin, if you keep them hidden, they will control you. You win the battle by exposing them and letting Jesus give you peace.

Prepare for War

Find a mentor and come to him or her with your enemies of fear, doubt, worry, and anxiety. In most cases, your mentor should be a mature Christian of the same gender. Recent trends of gender confusion issues may go against this council. This person will help you with your problems. They must not be a gossiper, sharing your problems with other people.

When you have doubts and questions (and you will), ask Jesus your questions, and bring your doubt before Him. Ask Him to increase your faith.

When you feel afraid, filled with anxiety, or worry, take it to your mentor. Ask for prayer and counsel on how to kick these enemies of the faith to the curb.

Chapter 7
Minister in Your Affliction

"But He said to me, 'My grace is sufficient for you, for My power is made perfect in weakness.' Therefore, I will gladly boast all the more in my weaknesses so that Christ's power may rest on me." (2 Corinthians 12:9)

In the last chapter, I wrote about my setbacks and dealing with doubt. Those were dark times in the Laurel Center. In this chapter, I want to highlight the high points there and when I finally came home. It wasn't all bad. A lot of it was good.

God can use you even in your weakness and affliction. I believe He can use you more as you struggle, and He strengthens you. People are watching you. They imagine what you go through, rarely asking about it, but seeing your faith and faithfulness to the Lord. The Holy Spirit uses that to minister to others through you.

If you've got a pulse, God has a plan.

When I lay motionless on that hospital bed in the Reading Hospital, experiencing the loss of control of my body and grappling with the possibility that my part in ministry was over, that hurt the most. I lost my identity as far as I was concerned. I didn't know what was next. I was alive, but that was all.

Boy, was I wrong. Never stop believing that Jesus can minister through you. If you've got a pulse, God has a plan. Trust in Him to write the next chapter of your story for His glory. I know His plans for me have provided opportunities to minister to others.

Coming Home

Many people were involved in bringing me home from the Laurel Center. At first, I was apprehensive about coming home. I had several major concerns. My parents live in a rural area, and if there was a medical emergency, I was farther from medical facilities than I was at the Laurel Center.

I also didn't know much about home healthcare. One thing I did know, though, was that coverage could be spotty with nurses missing shifts. Whatever coverage we didn't have, my aging parents and family would have to cover. These were the two main problems I could foresee.

God blessed me with great parents who care deeply for me. They wanted to bring me home despite these challenges. My mom was still working in Tupperware and at a tax office. My dad had just retired from his job at a federal prison as a carpentry trade instructor. He was willing to cover my care if we did not have a nurse.

My parents sacrificed time and resources to bring me home.

When we were sure I was coming home, my dad took a large deck he had built and turned it into a sunroom. This is where I would stay when I came home. In the beginning, we thought it was a large space, but I have filled it with all my equipment and everything we need for my care. I can't imagine what we would do without this space.

All these moving parts came together according to God's will for me. My parents sacrificed time and resources to bring me home. The new nurses came to our house to take care of me. Vital and valuable resources were prepared for my care. The Lord's hand was in it all, and the ministry opportunities I would have at home were greater than at the Laurel Center.

Preaching Galore

When I got home after all the adjustments to keep me home, I was privileged to preach about eleven times. I went to churches throughout my section. It was a joy to be back in the pulpit, whether I set my wheelchair behind one or preached from in front of the stage. I felt like I was back. I knew I was doing what Jesus had made me to do.

One of my struggles in the hospital and rehab was that the thing I loved to do the most, I didn't know if I could ever do again. I didn't have my voice until my second week in rehab. How can a person fulfill God's call to preach without a voice?

When I came home, I didn't know if I would get opportunities to preach very often, but that first year of preaching so much, being welcomed home in my section, was life.

After the first year, I didn't get to preach as much, but I cherish and enjoy every opportunity I am given. Perhaps pastors were dealing with the COVID-19 pandemic, shutting down their churches for public safety for a time, and concerned about my health with a compromised immune system. Writing books, blogs, and ministering through the written word is good, but I love to preach and teach in person using my voice.

However, I don't like to put churches or ministers on the spot. I'm not good at marketing myself. Ministers should not be good at marketing themselves, just preaching the gospel. I don't want to make people feel bad if they don't have me come to their church. God will take care of me and provide opportunities.

I don't feel I could pastor a church at this time. I have some days where my nerve pain is so great that I could not commit to being a full-time pastor. I know there would be times during the week with my schedule that I could not fulfill the time I want to devote to a church.

Even some Sundays are a trial for my parents and me to get to church. Depending on the weather, we miss some services even on days I feel great. Having a wheelchair makes it hard to get around in some places. Doing home visits as a pastor would be a challenging task. I would love to pastor again, but until the Lord heals me, it would be unethical for me to take on a church and not be the best pastor I could be.

Still, I thank God for every ministry opportunity I receive. I have a desire to preach to any church that invites me. Along with the written word, I participate in several preaching opportunities, Bible studies, and life groups.

My Big Realization

At first, I could not understand why I became paralyzed. I believed that the devil attacked me, but I didn't know why. I was faithfully preaching and teaching God's Word to my congregation and loving the people. It was a small congregation, and I didn't know how influential I was as a pastor and leader.

I preached a message on one of the seven churches in Revelation, prophetically believing—closer to the beginning of my paralysis—that our church was small but had great spiritual power. I said there was an open door for us and that we must have the courage to walk through it.

I preached a series on holiness at the end of 2012. I spoke about it that Thanksgiving at our dinner table casually, but my grandma challenged me to write a book based on the series. I told her I was too busy with my other ministry duties, but I felt the Lord calling me to write the book. I started writing it about a month before my paralysis.

> I may have been more trouble to the devil than I thought.

It seems obvious now, but at the time I didn't put these pieces together. I may have been more trouble to the devil than I thought. The influence of the messages and ideas I was preaching and teaching may have aggravated him.

I'm not big headed enough to think that I matter that much to him. I don't believe that every problem that believers have is because the devil is after each of us. But I do feel that someone in the evil spiritual realm had enough of me or wanted to make an example of me.

I have come to the realization that every pastor is a target for the enemy. The devil, or his demons, tried to shut me up. They were tired of the messages I was preaching and the material I covered as I taught. They put a hit on me.

They just have one problem—they don't have the authority to finish the job. They tried to shut me up, but with every word I write, every message I preach, every lesson I teach, and every life group I lead, I'm kicking the powers of evil in the teeth.

And by God's grace, I will not quit.

Are you dangerous, demolishing the works of the enemy? Are you on his hit list? Every Christian needs to be a threat to the enemy. How can you be more effective at destroying Satan's works in your world?

Trust in the Lord

God is teaching me to be patient, humble, to ask for help, and to worry less about what I can't change. And what I can't change in this season has a long list. It's also teaching me a spiritual lesson, to rely more and more on the Lord. I know we're supposed to grasp these core fundamentals of our faith at any stage of our lives, but when you can't do for yourself, you learn it whether you want to or not. Do you mentally accept doctrine without realizing its implications?

Trusting in others to help me with my routines and everything I need is teaching me to trust Jesus for all His blessings and promises. When I could move for myself, take care of myself, and do everything I wanted to do, I thought I understood trusting in the Lord. But now that I trust in others for almost everything, the Lord is showing me what true trust really is.

Is there something you think you have control over in your life? Even the next breath you take happens because of the grace of the Lord. I realize how much my life is in His hands now that I have no allusion of control. I have had to trust nurses, my parents, and others for every little thing. Jesus decides everything about your life.

He is sovereign over every part of your life. You can argue with Him, throw temper tantrums when you don't get what you want, and turn your back on Him, but that doesn't change His sovereign care for you.

I knew all this before my paralysis. At least, I had a head knowledge of it. Now, I experience God's sovereign grace and care over my life with every breath.

You can learn many facts about God academically, but you learn so much more when you must experience and trust in His unfailing love and grace for you. God has never let me down. Every experience confirms how much He loves me. I never had to rely on Him so much before all this. Until you learn to trust in God's sovereign hand on your life, you will not know what you think you know about Him.

How would you rate your trust in the Lord from 1-10? Do you have weak spots in trusting Jesus? In what parts of your life have you not given Him complete control?

Searching for Purpose

I am almost afraid to admit this in writing, but those first couple of months after my paralysis, I was searching for my purpose. At Hershey Medical Center and MaGee, there wasn't much I could do toward ministry. I was receiving ministry from others.

I have a hard time taking a rest or realizing what God is doing in me personally. But this didn't feel like rest to me. It felt as though I was being sidelined by the devil. Without a voice until I got to rehab and to MaGee, I could not preach. I could barely communicate with anyone.

I could not type on my computer or look through my commentaries and other ministry resources. I couldn't study the Bible. My mom read Scripture to me while I was in the hospital, but I couldn't do anything for myself. I am not used to such vulnerability. One of my friends bought me software that takes my speech and turns it into text. The same software allows me to operate my computer without assistance. I will talk about it in the final chapter.

What if I could never speak again? What if I couldn't communicate God's Word to people? I felt lost for the first time since feeling called to ministry. Ministering to others was my purpose in life, or so I thought. It appeared I had to do some soul-searching during this time.

This might have been the biggest struggle of all since I became paralyzed. I didn't realize that *existing* was all I had to do to be loved by God, my parents, or loved ones. They were just happy I was *alive*. I have never really understood that kind of love before this.

I had counted on having worth through what I could do for others, what I could teach them, or how I could lead them, but for the first time in my life, I was the one who needed others to help me. I needed ministering to and help to survive.

Existing was all I had to do to be loved.

I learned of the goodness and humanity of others. It's not that I didn't know this before, but I was now keenly aware of it. And I finally understood what it means to love a person for who they are not what they can do for others.

I found my emotions much more active after my paralysis. Just the little things would send me into a fit of crying. When people took care of me, I gave it much more attention and thankfulness. When I heard stories of other people becoming paralyzed or having any illness or sickness, it turned my thoughts inward and my compassion for others outward. Perhaps I was learning how to be a better minister through this experience.

Do you know your purpose and ministry? How is God ministering through you right now? Do you hear the Spirit and follow His lead? Every Christian has a ministry and at least one gift of the Spirit. What are yours? Are you using them?

God's Work in Your Affliction

How should you understand your affliction? Is it a test from God? Does God discipline His children through sickness, disability, and affliction? I've covered some false doctrines on this topic in an earlier chapter. How you see your affliction and what the Bible says about it can be a weapon against fear and doubt.

The way we speak about our affliction matters. Words have power. The way you think about your situation comes out in the words you speak. This doesn't mean you have pronounced your affliction over yourself. Believe God's Word over you instead of speaking from doubt, fear, and worry.

Did God bring your affliction on you as a trial to teach you something? God didn't bring your affliction on you. He doesn't teach you a lesson by bringing affliction upon you. To this day, I search for reasons as to why I became paralyzed. Did I do something to my body? Was I doing something wrong?

When my neurologist explained that a random antibody attacked my spinal cord below the brainstem and then disappeared within a day, I smiled and said to him, "That's the worst case of a hit-and-run I have ever heard of." I couldn't even get a smile out of him. His analysis put many of my thoughts to bed. It was random in his words, but could I have avoided it with some other action? It didn't appear so.

"That's the worst case of a hit-and-run I have ever heard of."

God gives us assurances as we walk this path. He whispers His grace in our ear. You acknowledge your affliction, but you speak in faith over it. You declare the promises of God over it. This simple act is powerful in the spiritual realms. The enemy can't stand against God's powerful Word spoken by His faithful child. Let that power grow inside of you. Trust it instead of your mountain affliction. God is greater than your mountain, than your affliction.

The only time God brought sickness to His people was when they doubted His power to provide for them in the wilderness (Num 21:6-9). Their disobedience brought God's discipline through disease and death. Part of the Old Covenant promised sickness when Israel did not stay committed to God (Deut 28:15-68).

The only time I can think of where God judges His disciples by striking them dead is when Ananias and Sapphira lied to the Holy Spirit and Peter called them on the carpet (Acts 5:1-11). But He does not bring afflictions on His children under the New Covenant. While God may not bring affliction upon you to teach you a lesson or punish you, He can use your affliction to draw you closer to Him. I have grown closer to the Lord and have learned by experience His attributes. He has not told me, though, that I committed a sin or did something He disliked, or that He brought this paralysis to punish me.

Do you realize how the Holy Spirit ministers through you to others? Do you serve others instead of yourself? How can you be more effective for Jesus?

Rekindle Your Passion and Purpose

I have always believed that as long as you are alive, God has a purpose for you. When Elijah experienced a great victory on Mount Carmel, Queen Jezebel crushed his sense of purpose. She made it sound like she was in control of Israel.

Elijah ran into the wilderness, depressed and defeated. God took him to Mount Horeb where He first revealed Himself to Israel. He tested Elijah's ability to know His presence. A strong wind, earthquake, and fire ravaged the mountain, all signs of God's presence. Elijah didn't come out of the cave until he heard the still small voice, the gentle whisper, of the Lord (1 Kgs 19:12).

Twice God asked Elijah, "What are you doing here?" (1 Kgs 19:9, 13). What did Elijah expect God to do there? Elijah was ready to throw in the towel. He had served God faithfully for many years, but he was broken down, out of steam, and severely burned out. He had lost God's vision for Israel. It was time for God to raise up another prophet in his place.

Nobody serving the Lord gets a pass because of an affliction.

You might feel that God is finished with you. Maybe you've given your all and think your affliction has set you free from His call and purpose for you. But nobody serving the Lord gets a pass because of an affliction. I had no excuse to stop ministering just because I became paralyzed. God doesn't quit on you. He saw this coming.

God gave Elijah a renewed purpose (1 Kgs 19:15-16) and changed his perspective. Elijah thought he was the last loyal prophet in all Israel, but God revealed that there were seven thousand prophets who had not bowed their knee to the false God, Baal.

What's your passion, and how can you minister to others? Do you fit in your church ministries? Are you in the wrong ministry—one that doesn't agree with your passion? If you don't fit, perhaps God is calling you to start a ministry within your church, or alongside churches. Be Jesus to the people around you because they need to see Him instead of you.

What Can You Do?

You are reading about my experience, my affliction. What trial or affliction are you suffering? How can you use your situation to glorify Jesus and put Him front and center before others? There is a saying often referred to at the time of this writing, "Don't let a crisis go to waste." I ask you, how can you minister for Christ in your weakness, affliction, or trial?

Jesus wants to minister through you. Make the most of every opportunity (Gal 6:10; Eph 5:16; Col 4:5) to do good and share your testimony. Let the Holy Spirit do what He wills through you and your experiences. Faithfully serve the Lord and give Him all the glory for His blessings and mercies.

I spent five weeks in a school for the blind in Pittsburgh between my junior and senior years in high school. I confounded one blind man there as I was open about my faith. He could not understand why I still trusted in Jesus despite being legally blind from birth. I explained to him what I have always believed—that our trials and afflictions are surface conditions, but faith in Christ is an unshakable anchor under the surface of our lives.

> Our trials and afflictions are surface conditions, but faith in Christ is an unshakable anchor under the surface of our lives.

No matter my affliction or trial, my faith in Christ remains. He had my allegiance before paralysis, and He has my allegiance now. I will not waiver just because of a few setbacks. He saved my life for eternity, and He saved my life on September 25, 2013. As long as I live, I will dedicate myself to serving Jesus. He deserves my faithfulness.

A great cloud of witnesses surrounds you and me, showing the same faithfulness to Christ (Heb 12:1-2). What trial do you suffer for Christ? What's your testimony of faithfulness to Jesus? We owe it to Jesus to be faithful and serve Him with our whole being. Let us be faithful to the end and hold each other accountable.

Kids Ministry

Two or three times a year I get to preach in kids ministry. My favorite part of the service is when they come and pray for me. I am impressed by their faith. I understand why Jesus talked about the faith of a child (Matt 18:5). Some of them ask me what happened to me, but none of them demand this information to pray.

I remember one boy who saw me for the first time; he looked at his mother and said, "We need to pray for him." Most adults don't have that intuition and faith that prayer will make a person well. It's not usually our first reaction to pray. We've been taught by the world to do other things first, but prayer should always be our first reaction.

We can learn a lot from kids.

We can learn a lot from kids. The children's pastor asks me to teach the kids, but many times the kids teach me. They take me back to a place of pure trust in the Lord. They don't use big words when they pray. They don't have a master's degree like me. But when they pray, they believe. People who intercede for us do not need our doctor's diagnosis, a detailed explanation of what to pray, or a list of the reasons doctors and scientists can't fix it. Let the

Holy Spirit use people who intercede for you in His way. He will tell them what they need to pray.

I was not good at preaching or ministering to kids. I didn't consider it my calling. When I prepare messages and teachings for them, it forces me to change my vocabulary from big words to more simple ones, to not use Christianese, and to praise God for teachers and children's pastors who do this regularly.

I spend more time on kids' messages than those for adults. The whole time I prepare, I am thinking to myself, "How can I explain this without the shorthand of theology or without big words?" I want to have the same content that a person with a master's can understand without the academic words to hide behind. Kids teach me how to preach the gospel and teach the Bible to every age. I come to minister to them, but they minister to me.

New Ministry

God called me at seven years old to serve as a pastor. Everything in my life from that moment until I received credentials moved toward that end. Sudden paralysis was the first time I questioned my call. I wondered in that hospital bed, "How can God use a preacher who cannot speak?" But God restored my voice in His time.

He gave me a new ministry as a chaplain to a room full of people hungry to hear the messages He placed on my heart. When I came home, He gave me many opportunities to preach and share my story with congregations in my area. But preaching and teaching were not the only ministries God had for me.

The call never left me, but it has changed in the ways I share it. The messages about holiness found a different medium. I began learning how to perfect my writing skills, communicating in another way I had not seriously considered. The call to communicate God's Word has never changed, but the way I communicate has taken on new mediums.

A friend of mine wished to co-author books with me. We began doing this together in Bible College. He bought my first version of Dragon NaturallySpeaking, a speech to text software that transformed my spoken words onto the page of Microsoft Word. It liberated me to continue ministry in new ways. Sure, I wrote sermons all the time, but this allowed me to write blogs and books that could reach anyone on the Internet.

These new avenues of ministry required me to learn a different skill set than I had before. I had to learn how to write good stories, write nonfiction with excellence, and consider the people who would read what I wrote. I have learned more than I can imagine about the writing industry ever since, but I have much more to learn.

My sudden paralysis shocked me, but it was no surprise to God. He teaches me how to serve Him with every avenue of ministry He shows me, and He can do the same for you. We must have courage to embrace every opportunity to do Jesus's work. If you are alive, He has work for you to do that will glorify Him. He lets you partner in His great work. All Jesus requires is our obedience.

> I didn't plan on doing any of this, but He knew all along what He would involve me in.

Step out in faith, and trust that He will empower and make you competent in every avenue of ministry for Him. When you fulfill your call with your gifts, expertise, talents, and willingness to serve Him, you are ministering just as I do.

Along with my ministry of writing naturally came a skill I acquired beginning in high school. I had to host my writing online to reach the most people I could. Blogs are hosted on websites. I had had a website from my time of pastoring in Shillington but had not set it up for blogging.

As I learned how to blog, I realized I would have to start another website for blogging. It was less of a learning curve because of the knowledge I already possessed about website creation and design. I started this website shortly after I came home. In April 2019, I began this new venture. This opened another facet of ministry for the Lord. I began helping churches with their websites. In 2020, a friend asked me to join the board of his nonprofit prison ministry. I built the website for this ministry, and that opened doors to help other ministries.

As I look back on how these things came about, I am amazed that the Lord has used me in these ways. I didn't plan on doing any of this, but He knew all along what He would involve me in. It has been my privilege—and will continue to be my privilege—to serve Him in whatever capacity He wants me to serve.

Can you turn what you like to do into a ministry to others? Are there new avenues of ministry you have turned down? Do everything you can to be an effective servant for Jesus. If you can't think of a way you can serve Jesus, ask people around you how they see you, and what ministry gifts they see in you. Sometimes their insight will help you see ministries you can't see for yourself.

God's Ministry through You

God has much for you to do as you wait for His complete healing. This is no time to sit on the sidelines. If you're not dead, God's not done. He has something for you to do now. Don't sit idly by while God does miracles around you.

Each of us must discover the paths of ministry God has for us. Most of my ministry now comes through the written word of blogs and books. God didn't change my calling to minister to His people as a pastor. I encourage others through my blogs and books. I still speak out and proclaim His gospel and healing promises. I do it more through the written word than the spoken word at this moment in time.

Don't give up on God's ministry through you. The medium may change, but the message never does. What can you do for Jesus despite your affliction? You can encourage others and build up their faith to see great things happen through them for God's Kingdom. Look for ways to minister to others. God receives glory when we put our faith into action.

The medium may change, but the message never does.

Don't let your affliction stop you from glorifying Jesus with your actions. Many times, when I get up to preach, I tell people that the devil tried to shut me up. The message he tried to stop is now in books, blog posts, and every sermon I preach. Though the devil tried to stop me from speaking, every time I declare God's goodness and the message Satan tried to stop, I'm kicking him in the teeth.

Confound the devil with your faith in action. Remember, your faith doesn't have an expiration date. The blind man in John 9 waited for thirty-eight years. The woman with the issue of blood waited twelve years. Jesus raised Jairus's twelve-year-old daughter. Blind people throughout the Gospels cried out to Jesus as He passed by, refusing to let their situation become their forever reality.

Stand on God's promises. Abraham and Sarah waited twenty-five years for Isaac, the promised son, to be born. Job refused to curse God and die (Job 2:9). The writer of Hebrews spent an entire chapter talking about those who believed in faith without seeing God's promises (Heb 11). He says in that chapter that the world was not worthy of them, and they didn't see the fulfillment of the promise in their lifetime (vv. 38-39).

God wants you to serve Him and has provided a mission field for you. Living in this world is all about ministry. We are not here to serve ourselves. We are here for the Lord's purposes. Even if you have a nine-to-five job, it's your sacred duty to serve the Lord through evangelism and to help others. You provide godly wisdom, are salt and light to people who would not otherwise consider Godliness. You are a breath of fresh air to them.

See God's Hand in Your Healing

God works in the mundane and the miraculous. We must see His handiwork all around us and in us. How many times have we not stopped to admire the beauty of the sunrise and sunset? The finger of God has created everything we see. How can we be grateful and pour out our praise for our healing if we don't recognize His handiwork and the rest of His creation?

We thank God for the wonderful things He does. How can you notice even the smallest of changes in your affliction and condition if you cannot see the everyday beauty and blessings God has made? We must appreciate what God is doing all around us.

If we can recognize God's hand in our miraculous healing, we must recognize His hand moving behind the scenes of our affliction. Jesus must receive praise and thanksgiving for everything He does. Let us always take the time to realize the little things Jesus does, not just the magnificent miracles He performs in our bodies, healing His creation.

Prepare for War

Ministry is not for the "professional" pastor, the elite, or the full-time preacher. *Every* Christian does ministry. You do it in your home, in your school, at your job, and on the streets. You minister to family, friends, coworkers, fellow students, and even strangers.

Don't stop ministering to everyone you meet. You don't know your influence and reach. Take your reputation and witness seriously as a representative of Jesus. Let the Holy Spirit speak through you.

Jesus has empowered you to be a minister of His good news. What are the untapped areas of ministry in your world? How can you be even more effective for Jesus?

Chapter 8
Step toward Your Healing

"Now faith is the assurance of things hoped for, the evidence of things unseen." (Hebrews 11:1)

When I came home, I had many positive experiences including steps toward my healing. We took care of some health issues that were concerns when I was in nursing homes. Coming home is a healing experience in itself. There's no place like home.

How do you handle small steps toward your healing? Do you give glory to God for them? Do you see them as God ministering to you? Sometimes, we don't notice the little things God is doing in our lives and in our bodies along the way to healing.

As I tell some of my story, you will see God involved in the little things in my life. The same is true for you. Don't read this as someone else's story, as merely a story of interest. Read it as a testimony that increases your faith to see the little and big miracles God does in our lives.

Three Hospital Visits

Within the first three months of being home, I had three hospital visits and two surgeries. They were necessary to make me healthier than I have been since being a quadriplegic. I came home with a hole in my belly. My weekday day shift nurse was mortified. It led directly to my stomach and bile spilled onto my skin.

In the nursing home, the solution was to put a tea towel over it. This kept my clothes from staining and protected my skin from being burned by the bile. This hole should have closed naturally after two weeks. When it didn't close, they told me I needed to lose weight. After several pounds, they still said I needed to lose weight.

My home care nurses refused to continue this practice. We visited a surgeon who examined the hole. He found I had a fistula, a permanent hole in my belly that required surgery to close it. Two weeks before the scheduled surgery, my belly started bleeding, so we went to the hospital. After an endoscopic procedure (putting me to sleep and putting a tube down my throat into my stomach), the surgeon decided it was a minor bleed. He kept the schedule for the original surgery.

The other issue when I arrived home was my first trach change. My weekend day shift and night shift nurses changed it. They could not understand why I had such an adverse reaction to changes. After changing it for the first time since I was home, they had the most horrified reaction.

One nurse looked at the other and said, "They're not supposed to go that way." She immediately encouraged my mom to schedule an appointment with an ENT (Ear, Nose, and Throat) surgeon to figure out how to fix the problem. My ENT examined me in his office and concluded he needed an operating room to look deeper.

He wanted to do a quick thirty-minute look without anesthesia. I asked him if it would hurt. He replied, "Oh yes. It will really hurt." I asked to be put under for the operation. He was disappointed, as this required an anesthesiologist and extra steps. I try to minimize pain any way I can.

After a one hour and forty-five minute surgery, he came out and informed my parents, "It's by the grace of God your son is still alive." When Hershey did the tracheostomy, they didn't sew down the skin flaps from the hole they made to put the trach in. As I mentioned earlier, since they did the tracheostomy bedside instead of in an operating room, the trach was placed into the side instead of center of my neck.

My ENT surgeon could only do so much to try to fix it. Every time my trach was changed, I could have died. Pulling the trach out tore the skin flaps again. Torn skin could have fallen into the hole and covered my trachea, and the new trach would have sealed it over my breathing tubes. Looking back on my paralysis, I could have died around forty times!

I thank God for my nurses and the other medical professionals who protected me from further danger and brought me closer to better health. Today, I'm the healthiest quadriplegic I can be. I quip with my neurologists and doctors that I'm "as healthy as a quadriplegic ox."

Let Nothing Steal Your Hope

Hope is essential to our faith. It is the fuel that gives our faith wings. The darkness comes to steal your hope. Satan knows that if he takes your hope, you will have nothing left. There is no hopeless situation on this earth. For it to be hopeless, it would mean God cannot reach or change it. Such a thing does not exist.

> There is no hopeless situation on this earth. For it to be hopeless, it would mean God cannot reach or change it. Such a thing does not exist.

Many things give me hope. God's promise of healing gives me hope. The Bible gives me hope. Reading the stories of paralyzed and blind people, and their healings by Jesus in the Gospels, gives me hope.

Reading statements like, "Jesus Christ is the same yesterday, today, and forever" (Heb. 13:8) fuels my hope. The fact that my salvation, faith, and hope cannot be taken by anyone or anything feeds my hope.

Hearing testimonies from others who have been healed gives me hope. I know that if God did something amazing for them, He can do the same for me. Reading verses like Luke 1:37 that declare nothing is impossible with God give my faith a foundation to stand on. Trusting God for everything in my life, seeing that He has never let me down and never failed in any of His promises keeps my hope alive. God can heal my impossible paralysis.

My neurologists have already told me they can't do anything more for me but manage my pain; this proves to me that my ultimate hope and faith should rest in God. He made the body, and He has complete knowledge and power over it. Thinking about the blessings I have in Christ every day empowers my hope.

Faith outlasts the circumstances of life.

I realize that my condition could actually be worse, and when doctors made me aware of some health conditions that usually accompany paralysis of my kind, that made my heart grateful to Christ and strengthened my hope and faith in Him.

So many things bolster my hope and faith. You know how they tell you that when you're climbing a rope, don't look down? I tell myself not to dwell on my paralysis and pain. I try to look up to Jesus and focus on His promises and faithfulness to me. When I feel unbearable pain, I pray. Jesus has been such a Helper to me that I cannot blame Him or fault Him.

When you talk about faith existing before your affliction, so too should you have faith during and after it. Also, talk about how your faith should not be shaken by momentary trials and afflictions. Faith goes deeper than circumstances. It is not swayed by them. Faith outlasts the circumstances of life. Only you can give up your faith. Nothing can take it from you.

I'm sure you have noticed this in your affliction, but Jesus is always there for you. He doesn't become silent when your affliction begins. You and I can call on Him no matter the time of day or the reason. Jesus is faithful. He walks with us and sees down the road much farther than we do.

His blessings never cease. Despite afflictions and trials, Jesus never stops pouring His blessings on us. It's not that you have to strain to see them now, but that you probably took them for granted—or didn't notice them—before your affliction. The Bible says that God's mercies are new every morning (Lam 3:22-23).

We don't walk this path alone. Jesus suffered more pain than we will ever know. These truths may not seem true for you, but they *are* true—for everyone! Only Jesus has the monopoly on suffering. He pledges to be with us no matter what we face.

We cannot doubt or deny His love, loyalty, and presence. In the desert wasteland of our pain and affliction, we can never say we were alone, that no one else has suffered as we do, or that we don't have anyone to turn to. That is a blessing.

Speak in Faith

I'm far from a Word of Faith preacher, but there is power in what you say, what you speak over others, and what you speak over yourself. I don't know if you can speak sickness into your life, but I know you can declare the promises of God over your body. I know you can speak prophetically into your situation.

God's Word and promises are sure. When you speak them into your life, you speak prophetically and scripturally. Your body must come into alignment with God's promises. You come into agreement with God when you speak these healing promises over your body.

Speaking in faith on any of the promises of God does several things in the spiritual and natural realms.

- First, speaking in faith increases your faith and the faith of those around you. As faith rises, one of the two ingredients God uses to do miracles is readily available to Him.

- Second, speaking in faith declares God's Word and promises over your situation. It commands your body and your situation to align with God's Word.

- Third, it encourages you. Focusing on God's promises takes your attention off your pain and your affliction.

There's no downside to speaking in faith. What if your declaration doesn't make your healing happen? That's not up to you. God does the miracle in His time. Whether reality comes into focus for your affliction as you declare God's goodness and promises over your situation or not, your faith is not subject to time and circumstance.

When you speak in faith, you are simply obeying. God only calls you to have faith; He doesn't tell you to heal yourself. That is up to Him. When you speak in faith, you do your part. I cannot heal myself, but I can speak in faith and lay the groundwork for God to heal me at His command. You come into agreement with God's Word, and He does this sovereign miracle in you when He wishes.

It didn't take long to see God is working in the background of my life, orchestrating events I could not have imagined. I would meet caring nurses and be home with my family. God already knew what would be best for me.

Being Home Is Better

Living in hospitals and nursing homes was the only way to deal with this immediate paralysis. My dad wanted to wait until he retired to think about bringing me home. He had great wisdom because now he is a regular caregiver while I am home.

Nothing is better than being home. I am so thankful I get to be around my parents, my sisters, and my nieces and nephew. It's good to be around family. Something about being around everyone is comforting even when I am in pain or there is an emergency.

> God only calls you to have faith;
> He doesn't tell you to heal yourself.
> That is up to Him.

I grew up in this house, and I love being here. I always miss home when I'm away from it. I think it helps my psychological and physical health to be here. When I came home, we took care of some physical issues, which I've already written about. I love being here.

Sure, I was getting care in the other places, too, but while I am home, my parents don't have to travel to see me. I can go anywhere I wish in my van. These were not options when I was living in nursing homes. Truly, there's no place like home.

There is no substitute for being at home. Just getting to participate in the lives of my family members is more than worth the challenges we faced bringing me home. I feel so thankful to my parents for bringing me home and to my nurses for helping me stay home.

I Don't Do It Alone

When my paralysis happened, I woke up that night in a hospital and heard the reassuring voices of my parents, my sister, and my congregants. Since then, I trust in the support of my parents and family members, the kindness of Christian friends, and the support system of doctors and nurses. Each of these groups has been a support system for me.

My family and nurses assist me daily. Doctors and neurologists hold regular appointments with me to assess my health condition. I love to tell them Jesus will heal me. They look doubtful, and I explain how surprised they will be when I walk into their office someday. I trust in God's Word because there is no other hope for me in this life or the next. God's Word is true.

I have even trusted our family dog. He ignores me for the most part, but one Saturday, a new nurse called off, and no one told us beforehand. My dad had gone hunting for the morning, and my mom was heavily asleep on the couch in my room. It was time to get me up in the morning for my medicine. The cuff on my trach, which closes off my voice at night, was still up. I could not get my mom's attention. So, I made a noise like raspberries with my lips.

I knew it wouldn't get her attention, but I was desperate. The dog came out to investigate the noise. When he came out, I stopped making it. He looked around and then went back into another room. I made the sound again, and he came out to investigate more. When he couldn't figure it out, he must have licked my mom's hand or something. Then she woke up and took care of me. Without the dog, there was no way for me to wake her.

Unlike some people with medical issues, my support system is vast. So many people are involved in my care. I certainly feel blessed by the Lord. When I was in nursing homes, I considered myself an advocate for quadriplegics who could not speak for themselves. I informed CNAs and nurses when what they were doing hurt or was not what they should do for a paralyzed person. I would tell them I hoped they were not doing it this way for the other quadriplegics.

My Dedicated Nurses

I want to avoid using my nurses' names, but I must tell you what a blessing they are to me. Aside from having the professional skills to provide me with great nursing care, they have become my friends and part of our family. As much as I have invited them into my life, they have done the same for me.

I can be a handful. When you can't move at all, your body cries out for attention. And of course, I advocate for this body of mine. Some days I barely need moving at all, and other days it seems that every hour or two I need some movement.

Throughout the day, they provide me with meds, give me water, feed me, and bathe me. These are just a few things each of my nurses does for me. Throughout the night I need moving to avoid my skin breaking down. I must always keep drinking.

I am the most blessed by faithful nurses who barely take off time for themselves to make sure I am covered. They have sacrificed personal time and family time for me, and I will never forget that. They have blessed me not only with excellent medical care, but with friendship and kindness.

I have a day shift nurse who has been with me since the day I rolled through the door of my home. I have a night shift nurse during the week who has been with me since the very beginning. Another nurse worked tirelessly on my weekend nights for the first three years I was home.

I also have a few nurses who have worked with me for almost a year. And I have a nurse who goes with me on every vacation and works with me every other weekend. I will never forget these people. I am so grateful for everyone the Lord has sent me.

I know this will not be a condition I must live with forever. I often think of the ways I will be able to bless these people who have so blessed me when I am healed. Certainly, they will always be a part of my life. We have shared so much together. This does not scratch the surface of their dedication, or do them justice, but I only have so much space to tell you about these faithful, tireless servants who bless me every day I suffer this affliction.

My Parents

I am trying not to cry as I write about my parents. The doctors let my mother know what happened to me the day it happened. My parents, along with my younger sister, were there at the hospital the night I woke up. They have dropped everything for me more than just that day.

My parents faithfully came to visit me no matter where I was. Even when I was in Philadelphia, four and a half hours driving distance away from them, they were there regularly. When I was in Mechanicsburg and the medical staff weren't taking care of me, giving me a bath regularly, or even answering my call bell for long periods of time, my mom came and did everything from cleaning me up to making sure they did what I needed.

> I am trying not to cry as I write about my parents.

Even more since I came home, my parents have sacrificed to take care of me and keep me home. Lately, we have had less nursing care. Chalk it up to the pandemic, the economic issues in America now, or that people don't want to work if they don't have to.

My parents have had to take a more primary role in my care. Right now, every weekend seems to be without nursing care. My parents have stepped in and done my care over the weekends. However, they have their own lives. My mom is about to go back to work at her tax office, and she has her Tupperware business. My dad likes to hunt and keeps busy with gardening, taking care of the house, picking up carpentry jobs, and enjoying his retirement. Still they have dropped everything to help me—every opportunity they have. I feel like such a burden, but they don't let me feel that way.

I hope they will get some relief. We are beginning to get all our nursing shifts covered. It's hard for my parents and me to have broken sleep halfway through the night when they come to turn me the other way. I can tell they are tired the days they have to do my weekend care.

> Besides Jesus, my parents are the heroes of my story.

They don't just tell me they love me. They show it to me every day I am home. I have amazing, godly parents who have trained me in godliness since I was young. Even now they take care of *me* when I should be taking care of *them*. They will never know how truly grateful I am. They are my gift from God and my greatest blessing. Besides Jesus, my parents are the heroes of my story.

My Equipment

I came home to an electric bed that was much like the one I had at the Laurel Center. We looked for another bed because this one didn't have everything we wanted. Instead of cranking the bed up and down, which was hard on my nurses, we found a bed that has that feature.

The program we borrowed this bed from has an open borrowing policy like Ricky's Wheels where you borrow something until you don't need it anymore, and then you give it back for other people to use. My dad did some maintenance on the bed to make it the best it could be for our purposes. When the Lord heals me, I will give it back and pay it forward to someone else who needs it.

I came home with the same wheelchair I received at the Laurel Center. I still use it today. Other than a bit of maintenance here and there, it suits my needs. My mom found an electric lift at a sale, for much less than new lifts costs, to transfer me from my bed to my chair. It has been such a blessing. My parents have made many extra arrangements to have me home. I am thankful they have sacrificed many things to bring me home.

In 2015, while I was still at the Laurel Center, God blessed my parents with a wheelchair accessible Chrysler Town and Country van. The only drawback was that it was already fifteen years old. Nonetheless, we were so happy for the opportunity to get out when my parents visited. It was a wonderful blessing from the Lord.

I came home in that van, and we used it to go to church, attend events, go to doctor's appointments, and go wherever we needed to. There were a few issues with an older van. There wasn't great circulation for the air conditioning, and then it stopped working altogether. On hot summer days, we put down the windows. We just dealt with sweating and being hot.

Still, we saw it as a great blessing from the Lord. It gave me an opportunity to be out and about. I didn't have to stay cooped up in the house all the time. Before one of our vacations to Florida, we dropped the van off at a wheelchair accessible vehicle place in

Harrisburg. We wanted them to look at it and do some maintenance and tune-up.

We went on vacation, and a few days into it they called my mom and informed her that it had rusted out so badly on the bottom they recommended that we not use the vehicle anymore. Right where my wheelchair sat in the middle of it, the bottom was rusting out! At any time, my 430-pound wheelchair easily could have fallen through the floorboards.

It was time to find another wheelchair accessible van. The people who refit vans with wheelchair accessible features told us we needed to find a van not more than five years old. They could not refit a van older than that.

We did not have the money to buy a brand-new van. Mom and I began looking all over the Internet. I found a few, but they were not satisfactory. I was looking for already made wheelchair accessible vans—and by the way, even used ones are expensive!

If we were to find something that worked for us, it would come through God's guidance. My mom came upon a 2019 van local to us. The price seemed too good to be true. The first question she asked the dealer was why a 2019, the same year we were in, was back on the lot for sale.

They explained that it had been turned back in to them by the owner, who didn't have it very long. They test drove it and checked everything. We followed God's lead and got the van. We had to wait for a while for them to do the refitting, but then the van was ours. I could go to church, my doctor's appointments, and anywhere else I needed to go. I was glad to be out of my room every once in a while. God provided for all our needs. It was nice to have a blessing of a van that stays cold in the summer and warm in the winter.

Celebrate God's Goodness

We get this false idea that we celebrate God's goodness when we notice He is good. When we receive our blessing, we praise God. We worship God when He ends our affliction. That is not what the Bible teaches. We are to praise God at *all* times, in *all* seasons, without holding back.

With every breath and every word, we can celebrate the goodness of our sovereign King. How do you not see His continual grace and goodness being poured out on you? As long as you live, and after your life on this earth, God is pouring out His lavish blessings and goodness all over you and your situation.

I shock some people when I thank God for His goodness to me. They look at my physical circumstance, and it doesn't make sense to them. What am I thanking God for? For every breath I take. For every word I speak. For every opportunity to minister for His glory. For every sunrise. For every sunset. And for every moment in between.

> If you can't think of anything to thank God for and celebrate His goodness in your life, imagine what other people go through.

People even look more surprised when I say, "My situation could be worse." What could be worse than almost complete paralysis? My pain could be worse. My affliction could be worse. I could be dead. There are people with more debilitating afflictions even than this.

If you can't think of anything to thank God for and celebrate His goodness in your life, imagine what other people go through. Put yourself in their shoes. Then thank God and celebrate His goodness that you do not suffer as others do. If that feels wrong to you, I give you full permission to thank God that you are not in my shoes.

A Typical Day

Every morning, I wake up at 8:00 a.m. to take pills and have a breathing treatment. After my pills comes a bed bath followed by breakfast. Then I get on my computer until it's time to wean off my vent. Weaning is when I breathe on my own using a Passy-Muir Valve (named after the inventor). This makes me breathe in through my trach and out of my nose and mouth. It also makes it a little harder for me to breathe to strengthen my lungs.

I eat lunch after that having my afternoons and evenings free until my evening routine. Such routines are very important. Since I don't move, these routines keep my body normalized. This is something people don't consider when their body does these things automatically.

Someone must feed me for every meal, whether a nurse or my parents. Sometimes people don't realize that I can't do anything on my own. If it doesn't involve using my voice, I need help to do it. It's not that I don't like other people doing for me, but I feel like I'm such an imposition. I'm the kind of person who likes to do things for myself. Much of that attitude comes from being legally blind since birth.

I hate the words people use for my condition. I don't like "handicapped" because it implies I am less than able to do something everyone else can. I don't like "disabled" either because it reminds me of how little I can do for myself anymore. I don't have better words to use. I suspect I'm not alone in how I feel about these words. "Challenged" implies I can overcome the challenge. Until Jesus heals me, I cannot overcome the challenge of paralysis. You are free to use any of these words since I cannot offer better ones. But these are the reasons I don't like the words people have come up with to describe people like me. Just think of me as a person.

My evening routine deals with my bowel movements. We use medical procedures to make sure my bowels stay regulated and running smoothly. Since my muscles do not receive cues from my nervous system, these routines make sure I don't have health issues related to paralysis. Night medications help with extra pain and muscle relaxers to reduce spasms. We finally have most of my nerve pain under control.

On days with precipitation, my pain gets worse. Perhaps two or three days out of a month I will have no nerve pain. Human touch does not bother my nerves. But most fabrics do. We have found that when I have a blanket on, it soothes my nerve pain. I don't wear blankets because I'm cold. I can't feel cold and hot over most of my body. I wear them for nerve pain. I have muscle spasms when people move me around; Sneezing, coughing, and yawning can also cause spasms. They come with the territory of the spinal cord injury. I am blessed that my muscle spasms do not cause me pain.

Much of my day consists of writing blog posts, books, preparing sermons and Bible studies. I also design and maintain websites for various ministries. I watch TV every once in a while. My days are full of activity. I thank the Lord that I can do what I do.

Dreams and Visions

Soon after I arrived home, I experienced dreams and visions of myself preaching and teaching—moving around without paralysis! These dreams began about three months into my home stay. The Lord blessed me with what I understand is my future.

In one of them, I was talking with a pastor on a couch, waving my hands around like any good Italian does. I don't know what we were talking about, but that didn't matter. What mattered was that I was not paralyzed. I believe the Lord sends us dreams and visions of the possibilities in our lives. We should not consider them concrete.

Sometimes it's hard to distinguish personal desires from God-given dreams and visions. I wanted to be free of my paralysis. After I woke up, I evaluated whether these dreams were from God or from my desires. While I wanted to be paralysis-free, I could tell these dreams were from the Lord. I never imagined myself in the contexts of each of the dreams.

In another dream, I was the executive pastor under my mentor in Florida. These dreams were interesting because that was one of my personal dreams, to work with my mentor. This one was harder to evaluate because it could be that this is God's will for me in the future and my desire to work with my mentor coincided.

When you evaluate your dreams and visions, begin with your desires. Does the dream have any unexpected elements that could attribute it to God's will rather than yours? Is there any part of the dream you don't want for yourself? If there are parts you don't want, it could be a dream from God.

God wants to bless His children with things they cannot foresee as good in the short-term. However, we may not realize God's greater purpose in dreams that show us possible futures. Dreams given to Joseph in the Old Testament and Joseph in the New Testament did not look like the ideal future they would design for themselves.

Joseph in the Old Testament faced imprisonment for more than two years before he was catapulted to second in command of all Egypt. Joseph in the New Testament wanted to divorce Mary quietly before he had a dream of how Mary had become pregnant before marriage. Just because the dream does not fit our desires does not mean it's definitely from the Lord. Many of us have had nightmares that we didn't wish to ever happen to us.

Don't take your dreams as gospel truth. I did not take from my dreams the places I preached and taught as gospel but as a reaffirming truth that my paralysis does not last my entire lifetime. I don't know when Jesus will completely heal me. I don't know how. I just know that the experiences of dreams and visions since I came home have increased.

Find the overall truth in your dream from the Lord. The details may change as mine have, but the overarching truth of my dreams is that in every one of them, I am paralysis-free. So far, I have no reason to doubt the Lord is encouraging me that this paralysis is not forever.

Let Freedom Ring

Once I was home, I discovered amazing devices that helped me become more independent. My day nurse thought anything that would give me independence was good for my psyche. She applauded anything I found that would help me to this end.

I discovered Alexa, the Amazon based Echo devices and their ability to control things through Wi-Fi. We started with being able to control certain TV apps and anything under her system. Then I discovered the Fire TV Cube. This was a game-changer because it allowed me to control my TV on my own. With just my voice I could turn it on, change channels, adjust the volume, and still have the capability of the Alexa platform.

Then I discovered there were Wi-Fi switches and plugs that allowed me to control other devices besides my TV and the echoes. Now I could control the fans and fan lights, and other devices I could turn on and off. Without needing my nurse's help to control the TV and the cable box, there was just a little bit less I had to bother her to do.

My current wheelchair is a Cadillac of wheelchairs. Its a Sip & Puff system for driving and controlling the chair. Even without the use of hands and fingers, I control my wheelchair with my breath. A straw is attached to a computer system that understands and interprets my sips and puffs into the straw to drive the wheelchair.

It drives the chair, changes the seating, and can even be set up to be used like a remote control for a TV and other devices with the same technology. I'm not going to brag too much, but Superman had the same wheelchair with this setup. By Superman, I mean the actor Christopher Reeves who played Superman. An accident gave him the same quadriplegic paralysis I have. His Foundation is the supporting organization for the MaGee Rehab Facility I was so blessed by after Hershey Medical. He designed the programs that they taught us, and how to advocate for ourselves as quadriplegics.

The Sip & Puff system does not leave much room for error. Most people don't think of how much time it takes to slow down or stop. I sometimes let my dad drive from the joystick on the back of the chair to avoid crashing into people.

Over the year's I have become a better driver. I avoid hitting people at all costs. If the straw in my mouth detaches from any other part of the straw, I can't control the wheelchair. If I cannot use my breath through the straw, I cannot control this 430-pound vehicle. Even if I am going slow when the straw comes off the wheelchair I cannot stop it, slow it down, or turn side to side. I am helpless in a dangerous moving device.

I am blessed to still have my voice while operating the wheelchair. When this happens, I yell to my dad, "I have no control! I can't stop it!" He has learned over the years how to turn off the wheelchair quickly so it stops. Otherwise, I probably would have hurt some people, perhaps very badly.

So, I couldn't resist when my mom bought me a Superman T-shirt. Every time I wear it, I think of all the things I can do because of technology. Because of Dragon NaturallySpeaking, I can control my computer with my voice. Because of my wheelchair I can go many places I would've never thought of before. And because of the Amazon echo devices, I can control some parts of my room and devices.

Don't Waste Your Miracle

All four Gospels record Jesus feeding of the five thousand, but only John gives Jesus's words after collecting twelve baskets full of the remaining fragments. He tells them to gather the remaining fragments and curiously says, "that nothing is wasted." Why would Jesus be concerned with the extra fragments from His miracle of feeding five thousand men, probably over fifteen thousand people?[1]

There is a principle behind Jesus's statement about the fragments of bread. Here's what some scholars say about it. Some see the extra baskets as the bountiful and abundant blessing of the Lord.[2]

---

[1] Grant R. Osborne, *John: Verse by Verse*, Osborne New Testament Commentaries (Bellingham, WA: Lexham Press, 2018), 149-150. Grant Osborne offers a summary for the whole passage on the significance of Jesus's command to gather all the fragments in baskets. He mentions the Jewish custom, the abundance of the Lord, fulfillment of Jeremiah 34:31, a connection from the "lost" fragments to preserving the ones the Father has given Him (John 10:28-29; 17:11-12, 15), and the possible interpretation of the "twelve" baskets referring to the twelve tribes of Israel.
[2] Rodney A. Whitacre, *John*, vol. 4 of *The IVP New Testament Commentary*

Others see Old Testament echoes of this miracle.[3] Still others cite a Jewish custom for saving the fragment of bread.[4]

These are all acute observations by leading scholars. There's something to be said for Jesus placing such emphasis on the lost or wasted fragments. We must acknowledge the healing and miracle Jesus does in our bodies. Jesus's comment about no fragments being lost or wasted can be applied today by sharing your testimony of Jesus's healing in you, and any steps toward healing. Never give up the opportunity to give credit and praise to Jesus for every bit of healing you experience.

I take great joy in sharing with people the little steps toward healing I encounter. I will talk more about these in chapter 9. Little steps toward healing should excite us. We should see them as harbingers of God's complete healing to come.

Prepare for War

Do you leave time in your day to spend with Jesus? Do you have daily devotions that keep you in connection with Jesus? Don't plan your life with God around your day, plan your day around your life with God.

What does a typical day look like for you? The way you spend your time shows in your priorities. Your finances also display your priorities. What are your top three priorities? Does your time management and financial statement agree with the

---

Series (Westmont, IL: IVP Academic, 1999), 145; Leon Morris, *The New International Commentary on the New Testament* (Grand Rapids, MI: Wm. B. Eerdmans Publishing Co., 1995), 305-306; D. A. Carson, *The Pillar New Testament Commentary* (Grand Rapids, MI: W.B. Eerdmans, 1991), 270-271.
[3] Whitacre, *John*, 145.
[4] Carson, *Pillar New Testament Commentary*, 270-271.

priorities you listed?

Commit yourself to spending more time fulfilling an eternal mindset. What matters to God should matter to us. Are you living with unchristian goals or purposes?

Chapter 9
Be Encouraged for Your Healing

"Heal me, Lord, and I will be healed. Save me, and I will be saved, for you are my praise." (Jeremiah 17:14)

We all need encouragement in our struggles, sufferings, and afflictions. I want to personally encourage you in this chapter to keep your faith that God will heal you. He will restore what the enemy has stolen.

We often have trouble remembering all God's kind and good nature toward His children and the promises from His Word. Take these Scriptures and words of encouragement to heart. Let them increase your faith for the impossible—for the great things God wants to do in you. Nothing is too difficult for Him. Trust that God is not finished with you or your affliction.

Another Panic Attack

The second panic attack I have had since I was paralyzed came during the trach change shortly after I came home. For the first time, we realized I needed extra medicine when I had changes. This is why I tell you everyone has weak moments. Even a person with great faith can have moments of fear, anxiety, and worry.

I was wide awake for this trach change. My muscles weren't relaxed. I knew it was going to hurt when they changed it. All these facts combined to put me in a panic state. I pleaded with the nurse to let me die instead of changing it. Looking back on the experience,

I don't know why I had such an adverse reaction to one trach change. When I was in the nursing home at the Laurel Center, they changed my trach once every other month.

Could the panic attack be an attack from the enemy? Possibly. More likely it resulted from trach changes done over the years that caused me much pain or that didn't go well. Before we added medicine specifically for trach changes, I had to listen to loud music in my headphones and try to go to sleep before they changed it.

When you face setbacks—
and prepare yourself because
you *will* face them—
pray through them.

Two panic attacks since 2013 is not a bad record, but the way they make me feel and the possible panic attacks they can cause don't give me a good feeling about myself after it's over. I try not to sound like a crazy person.

That trach change did not go well, as I knew it wouldn't. I'd like to think I trust in Jesus and His strength and peace better than that, but everyone has these moments. Allow yourself moments of weakness. You are only human. Despite our fears, anxieties, and pain, Jesus gives us His strength and peace.

Pray through Setbacks

Your setbacks feel discouraging. They are not just physical. Setbacks affect us spiritually, emotionally, and mentally. A setback or relapse can change your mindset. It could turn you into a negative person instead of a positive one expecting to see good changes in your condition.

Setbacks can affect you relationally, turning you into a bitter or sour person. Naomi in the Bible had this problem. Losing a husband and her two sons changed her. Naomi's name means "pleasant," but after these damaging losses making her a widow without a man in that culture to provide for her, she went back to her home country of Israel in defeat.

Thus, she told everyone when she returned to call her Mara, which means "bitter." You don't have to be a Naomi. When you face setbacks—and prepare yourself because you *will* face them—pray through them.

Jesus loves you, and He proves His love by listening to your prayers and answering them. Talk with someone about your setbacks and how you feel. If you need to, talk with a professional Christian counselor. They will have helpful exercises and provide a listening ear to help you work through the issues that your setbacks, relapses, trauma, and turmoil are causing for you.

We all have ideas of what a perfect or "normal" person should be. Setbacks shatter those images. I would argue it's more dangerous not to talk to a Christian therapist about the issues setbacks bring up for you than to stuff your emotions and thoughts and let them fester until you blow up at someone. There should be no stigma attached to people who go to therapy in the Church.

Confuse the Enemy with Prayer

Every year we go to Florida for vacation I get the opportunity to preach at my mentor's church in Jupiter. In 2022, I preached on a Sunday morning and talked about the interruption Jairus must have felt when Jesus stopped to heal a woman with an issue of blood for twelve years. I focused on this interruption because sometimes we feel our affliction has interrupted our lives.

I asked how we react to that interruption, if we feel that we were first in line or that our healing is "put on the back burner." I talked about our emotional response to this. We could miss seeing Jesus do something amazing in that moment. One such moment happened that Sunday morning. At the end of my message during the altar call, I asked people with afflictions of all kinds to come forward for prayer.

As I have stressed throughout this book, having faith requires we take the first step toward prayer. Many people came up to the altar. I didn't do this deliberately, but my mentor mentioned as I prayed for people that our actions confused the enemy because a quadriplegic man was praying for the sick. He could not wait to see how many people God would heal through this action.

When we are obedient to the Holy Spirit, He can use our obedience to confound Satan. In these interruptions of our lives, God can do great things when we step out in faith, ignore our affliction, serve Jesus, and serve His Kingdom. God uses our faithfulness to be faithful to us. There's no time to waste. While you wait for your healing, you can bless others, and God can minister through you.

Recent Developments toward Total Healing

Celebrate God's goodness with every step toward healing. Every positive doctor's report, every new development in your affliction, and every indication that your affliction is sinking away is an opportunity to glorify God. Progressive healing is just as wonderful as immediate healing.

These opportunities give us a platform to speak of God's healing power. My most recent updates to my condition are a chance to praise God and share with other believers how my paralysis is changing. Glorifying God in updates also encourages believers to have faith that God is moving in their situations.

Since my paralysis in 2013, I have begun to feel cold and hot temperatures on my right leg and more sensitivity to touch and temperature changes in my left pec muscle. Quadriplegics usually don't have any feeling below their injury. I started getting some feeling back in the first month after my injury. These new feelings encourage me that God is working progressively in my healing.

> I have also been able to move slightly
> my toes in my left foot.
> I can see how God is preparing for His complete
> healing in my body.

I have also been able to move slightly my toes in my left foot. When I mentioned these new developments to my neurologist, he told us that neurologists have been noticing that nerves can reconnect after long periods of time. I believe this is the beginning of God healing me completely.

As I wean, my lungs have been getting stronger. This is preparation for my complete healing. My day shift nurse noticed that my vent has been receiving more air than it puts into my lungs. We asked the respiratory therapist if the vent was malfunctioning. After conferring with his colleagues, he said that the vent is working fine. Most likely I am breathing a bit and pushing more air into the vent.

Let this sink in, I can see how God is preparing for His complete healing in my body. My lungs are prepared to work on their own. The reconnect of my sensory nerves gives me hope that the motor nerves will soon connect to one another, and I will be able to move!

Don't Be Ungrateful for Healing

Meditate with me on the account of the ten lepers in Luke 17:11-19. Ten lepers meet Jesus on His way to Jerusalem between Samaria and Galilee. Samaria is full of a mixed population that the Jews looked down on. Additionally, Galilee had many Gentiles in it. This is important at the end.

These lepers stood at a distance and cried out to Jesus because the law did not allow them to be near anyone else. Their leprosy made them unclean, disallowed from entering the temple where God's presence dwelt. Leprosy also made them contagious to the rest of the community. So, they stood far off, in their uncleanness. However, that did not keep them from crying out to Jesus for mercy. They refused to tolerate their affliction any longer. They knew Jesus could change their circumstance.

Only Jesus can heal your affliction. Doctors cannot help you. Jesus is there. How have you considered other means of healing before Him? Recognize His presence, that He is with you, to heal you, to make you whole.

The lepers addressed Jesus as "Master," which only appears six times in Luke as a direct address (Luke 5:5; 8:24, 45; 9:33, 49; 17:13). This is not the word for "Lord." This is another word that the other Gospels use for the title "Teacher." The lepers treat Jesus with the utmost respect.

Jesus is worthy of my praise, and I address Him as the Master and Teacher over my affliction. He can do great things in my life. All I need to do is ask Him. Do I have the faith to be forward with Him and ask Him to do what I know He can do? If I don't call on Him or come forward, do I have the faith to trust that He can heal me? Why would I be silent?

Jesus does not ask the lepers about their faith. Crying out to Him from a distance showed their faith. *Jesus, you see my faith. You know what I need. I present myself before you, and humbly cry out for my healing today.* All ten of the lepers are cleansed after Jesus proclaims their cleansing and before they reach the priest for confirmation.

In this progressive healing, Jesus proclaims them healed. In their obedience, they are healed. Jesus heals them between the promise and its fulfillment. Only one came back to thank Him. My miracle is on the way. I obey Jesus as the miracle becomes my reality. I remain obedient and faithful to do everything Jesus tells me to do until my healing becomes my reality.

What is this account about? Healing? Certainly, the lepers were healed, but only because they obeyed Jesus's word. The full effect of their healing takes place on their way to see the priest. So, it also has to do with obedience. Jesus's word is confirmed in our obedience.

One out of ten lepers notices his healing when it happens, and he reacts by praising God loudly, running to Jesus, and falling on his face at Jesus's feet. When I see Jesus's healing in my body, the small steps of His healing, my response must be to praise and thank Him for the mercy He gives me.

This leper who praises God and thanks Him is a Samaritan. In the land of Israel full of privileged children of God, only a foreigner returns to thank Jesus for his healing. Am I willing for the rocks to cry out before I do? If Jesus did this for a foreigner, how much more me, one of His children? Do I realize the great privilege I have before Him?

The account finishes with a question that gives me pause. Jesus asks where the other nine lepers are. He expects praise and thanks from all ten. He deserves all my praise and thanks. I must not hold back as these nine lepers did. As a child of God, I have the privilege and opportunity to thank and praise Him for every little bit of healing I receive.

One more thing makes me pause. The final action word spoken by Jesus differs from the other action words. In Greek, it is a perfect verb. It sticks out in this account. Jesus says to this leper, "Your faith has made you well." The perfect verb is special. It is a continuing state based on a past event. This is the only leper who gets to hear Jesus proclaim a *continuing* state of healing.

> **This is the only leper who gets to hear Jesus proclaim a *continuing* state of healing.**

The others are healed, but I wonder whether their cleansing continued after they saw the priests. They were not grateful for their healing. Did they continue to receive healing? I believe that because of Jesus's mercy poured out, they did. But oh, how much better the cleansing of this Samaritan because of his grateful heart and mouth full of praise.

Jesus, may I be worthy of the healing You pour out in my life and on my body. May I always cry out to You, be obedient, and turn to praise and thank You for the healing You do in my body.

We must celebrate God's goodness and show gratefulness for every blessing He pours into our lives. If we lack gratitude, we may not expect to receive much more of His goodness. If we cannot steward our souls to be grateful for what He has already bestowed upon us, we should not expect to receive any more of His goodness and grace. As great as His healing in us, so should our praise and celebration of His goodness to us be.

Keep Glorifying God

If you haven't noticed the recurring theme on glorifying God through your affliction and its healing, let this be the exclamation point of this theme. Praising God before you experience your total healing exercises faith that He will heal you this side of heaven.

Yes, we will have new bodies with no defects, but we have seen that God's Word and promise is not only for healing after physical death; it is also for here in this life. Think of glorifying and praising God now in your affliction as practice for when He heals you.

Praising God is a healthy exercise to get our mind and heart off our affliction and onto our worthy Lord. He is our sovereign, and He deserves our praise no matter our physical state and health. Remind yourself of God's goodness, mercy, grace, and generosity toward you. There's always something to praise God about and thank Him for as we worship His holy name.

Hope and Faith

Our faith sustains us, but it comes on the wings of hope. I have described the difference between hope and faith this way: if faith is the engine that propels us forward even in times of doubt, fear, and apprehension, hope is the fuel that powers faith.

Our hope, which comes from the Lord, gives us faith that what God has promised will become our reality. We don't know how long until the Lord brings fulfillment to His promises. Hope gives us assurance that God will fulfill His promises for us.

Faith gives us unwavering trust in the Lord. He has never failed in fulfilling His promises. We look to the Bible to see how even over centuries God fulfilled His promises to Israel. He will not fail us. Hope lends itself to faith, and faith sustains us until God's promises become our reality.

Hope is the fuel that powers faith.

Our trust in the Lord is fueled by hope. That hope propels us to trust in the Lord when we walk through trials and dark patches. Our faith guides us through these difficult times and leads us to lean on Jesus and His promises. We know we will see what He has promised. We don't know the specifics, but we know He never fails. We stake our faith on that truth.

Faith Stands the Test of Time

When you hope for the future, you empower your faith to stand against the lies of the enemy. Your defiance of his plans to defeat you challenges him on the battlefield. Don't give the devil a foothold. Believe in God's healing promises and that He is healing you.

When we speak in faith and believe in our hearts that Jesus is healing us, we build up our faith. As of the writing of this book, I have been praying for my complete healing for nine years. I keep believing and trusting Jesus for that healing, refusing to give up on seeing Jesus heal me. I encourage and pray for others with afflictions.

Time and circumstance cannot confine our faith. Time does not hold faith in check. Don't give up on your healing because you have waited for a long time. Don't allow circumstances to smother your faith. Your faith is like an iceberg. Part of your body is above the water, blown and tossed by the waves of the sea and the winds. Most of your body is under the water, though, and your feet are firmly planted on the Rock that is Jesus. Though the winds and waves try to discourage you, the firm foundation of Jesus keeps you strong. Nothing can take away your faith. Nothing can destroy your reliance on Jesus.

Don't let time and circumstance erode your faith. Don't move from your Rock and salvation in Jesus. Stand on God's promises, and don't let the enemy deceive you or sway you from your firm foundation and your insistence that Jesus *will* come through for you.

Add Humor to Your Affliction

Sometimes we take ourselves way too seriously. I get it. Your affliction causes great pain. So does mine. You can't understand why you must go through your affliction. Neither can I. You don't want to go through your affliction anymore. Neither do I. People don't always take the best care of you. I've been through that, too.

> Sometimes we take ourselves way too seriously.

So why should you add humor to your life? I have always been a jokester. So, for me to have humor even in paralysis was a natural fit. Humor helps to lighten the mood. Instead of acting in a condescending way to your caregivers, use humor. Humor is universal and includes everyone in the joke. I have shared in this book only a fraction of the jokes and humorous moments I have had with caregivers, neurologists, and doctors.

Humor keeps you from bursting out in anger. It also keeps you from pushing all the problems or blame onto someone else. It makes your reaction lighthearted instead of condescending or blaming someone else. It can keep your more volatile emotions in check. Humor has many uses. You don't have to be angry or sad all the time.

Around Lent, I developed a joke that makes most people cringe, but it really is funny. I ask them, "What do you think I'm giving up for Lent?" Most of them don't hazard a guess. They just ask, "What?" I respond, "Walking," with a big smile. Many are afraid to laugh. A good rule of thumb is, if the person telling the joke makes a joke about himself, it's OK to laugh along.

You can laugh at yourself, your circumstances, or funny things that happen to you. They range from the ironic to things you laugh about so you don't cry. If you take everything too seriously, you'll always be looking around the corner. You'll feel cynical about life. If you believe in Jesus, your bad attitude gives Him a bad reputation.

People caring for you and around you already feel like they're walking on eggshells. Many people fear asking awkward questions about my paralysis. I open the door by telling them, "Go ahead. Ask me what you want to know. I am an open book." I throw in a joke or two, and it puts them at ease. Not adding humor may make it easier to blame God for your affliction, or even worse, to no longer trust in Him.

You can be a serious person. You can ask God questions about your affliction. You should have genuine emotions and conversation in prayer with Him. He's a big God. He can take your anger, fear, anxiety, and everything else you bring before Him. But a good sense of humor keeps you and others from an awkward relationship.

Wandering in Your Wilderness

On some days, I can understand how the Israelites felt in the wilderness, and why they responded the way they did. I feel like I am all alone, that nobody understands my pain level or what it feels like, and that I walk this path alone. But none of that is true. It is a deception of the enemy, covered up by pain and suffering. Our thoughts often deceive us.

Nobody understands pain. It's different for everyone, and no one really understands my reaction to it until they've had nerve pain. I try to avoid groaning and moaning because of it. Why is it that making noises seems to make the pain less? Most times I just close my eyes and remain silent. Prayer helps. Talking to Jesus reminds me of His greatness and companionship in pain.

Israel seemed to go from suffering to inflicting suffering on Moses and then questioning God. They paid for their blasphemies and rebellion. They tested God. He took them out of Egypt, the house of slavery, but they always wanted to go back there. I don't understand that. I don't understand Christians who want to go back to their former lifestyle. God has given us so much. Why would anyone give up God's blessings?

Our afflictions make us feel like wanderers in the wilderness, but those struggles don't have to be a wasteland. We can remember that Jesus is with us. We know He understands. He has been there. We can cast our cares upon Him (1 Pet 5:7). Focus on your inheritance in Christ, on the glory of heaven, and on His wonderful care for you. No one else can promise these things or understand your suffering.

Turn to God's Word

I have memorized Scripture since I was a kid. I find God's comforting words there. When you are in pain, it may be too much to look up comforting Scriptures. That's why I memorize them. I recall them when I can't handle my pain. I will pass on these Scriptures to you here.

One of God's healing promises comes from Psalm 103. I love that David commands his soul to bless the Lord (vv. 1-2). He does not blindly bless the Lord. He concentrates on the benefits of his relationship with God. I tend to concentrate on, "He heals your diseases," but it's best to read all of them because they all apply to us.

Our God is great because He forgives us, heals us, redeems us, crowns us with steadfast love and mercy, satisfies us with good things, and renews our youth (Ps 103:3-5). When I think of all God's good gifts, it makes me forget my affliction and pain. David spends the rest of Psalm 103 highlighting Israel's past blessings from God. When you experience your worst pain, enumerate God's blessing and benefits in your life.

Another personal favorite is Psalm 91. I realize it's a messianic Psalm describing Jesus, but we can apply some of its truths. All believers can dwell under the shelter of God's wings and say God is their refuge and fortress (vv. 1-8). I read verses 3-6 and think about all the ways the Lord has protected me from more harm. I thank Him that He covers me and protects me.

Job's faith amazes me. How could a man who did not even know of the devil's existence speak with such faith? Even when he says we should accept both good and evil from God (Job 2:19), God does not credit him as a sinner (1:22; 2:10). Job did not understand everything that happened to him but trusted in the Lord no matter what. I want to have that same faith.

In 2 Kings, King Hezekiah comes down with an illness, and Isaiah tells him he will not recover. Hezekiah turns to the wall in praise and weeps, and God promises to heal him (20:1-5). I know God will faithfully answer my prayers for healing. In the Scriptures, I see examples of His power and fulfillment of His promises. I see God's track record, how He has never failed to keep His people.

One thing that encourages me about Hezekiah's healing story is how God responds to our heartfelt needs. He moves in our circumstances and takes away afflictions. Sometimes, I feel like Hezekiah. I have worked for the Lord, but my healing is not based on my track record of faithfulness to God. He heals out of His storehouse of grace. I don't have to earn God's approval to be healed.

Another passage that encourages me in my weakest times concerns the father of a boy with an unclean spirit (Mark 9:14-29). His son had dealt with this demon for so long. The father must have been weary and hoping for deliverance for his son. When the disciples could not cast the demon out, the father's despair grew even deeper.

When he came to Jesus, his desperation poured out in a question about Jesus's ability to deliver his son. I can feel the deflation in his request, "If you can do anything, feel compassion for us and help us" (Mark 9:24). Jesus addresses his statement as a lack of faith. We all have moments where our faith is lacking. Perhaps you have had your affliction for a long time. Maybe you feel drained by the experience of carrying your suffering and burden and are tired from the fight.

Jesus met the father where he was, but He challenged the man to have faith.

Jesus met the father where he was, but He challenged the man to have faith. That call of Jesus that all things are possible for the one who believes invigorates my faith. With this father who was burdened by years of caring for a son who was harassed by a demon, my soul also cries out, "I believe! Help my unbelief" (v. 24). Jesus calls us to believe in moments of doubt, fear, concern, and lukewarm faith. We must rise to His call and believe that all things are possible.

In John 5, when Jesus encounters the invalid pulling himself toward the pool—trusting the wrong source of healing—He asks this profound question: "Do you want to be healed" (John 5:6)? Jesus's question penetrated to the heart of the issue. We can get used to the way things are. I know I sometimes get in the routine of dealing with my paralysis.

That question jars my faith to life. Am I really sick of my paralysis and the ways it limits me? Have I gotten used to it over time? I don't want to be like this man who offers excuses. I seek Jesus, the one who has all power to reverse this affliction and make me whole. I cry out to the Source of my healing. I don't want to settle for the routine of my affliction. Jesus has so much more.

I also look to the parable of the persistent widow (Luke 18:1-8). Jesus is nothing like the unjust judge. He is just, and He answers my plea out of His goodness, not out of annoyance. He challenges me to continue crying out for my healing. If I ever think I'm bothering Him, or if I become weary of persistence without healing, this Scripture calls me to continue asking Him. I know He hasn't forgotten me, but I don't want to give up just before my breakthrough.

Jesus calls me to trust Him and to seek increasing faith. At one point in Jesus's ministry, whatever cued the disciples' desire, they cried out, "Increase our faith" (Luke 11:5). I want my soul to rise up with the same request, an increase of the bit of faith I have. I want Him to pour out His grace and fulfill the lack in me.

I believe Jesus gives us faith to see great things happen in us. I look to the beginning of Hebrews 11 to remind me of what faith is and what God expects of me. The definition of faith encourages me to not focus on worldly results (Heb 11:1). My faith is a conviction in things I have not yet seen. My healing is coming whether or not I see it yet. Faith and hope combine to remind me that my healing is on the way. I must continue to turn my hope into assurance. I must remind myself that God rewards those who seek Him (v. 6). I must remember that God rewards faith that seeks Him for healing.

Be encouraged that Jesus began a good work of healing you, and He will carry it to completion (Phil 1:6). He will not let you down. He will not give up on you. Your impossible affliction must bow to the mighty name of Jesus. Paul reminds us that the Father raised Jesus from the dead and seated Him far above every power and every name that is named (Eph 1:20-21). If your affliction has a name, it must bow to Jesus.

Speak the name of your affliction and lay it at Jesus's feet. Proclaim it as part of your testimony, as a victory song, because Jesus has not finished your story. "But they conquered him by the Lamb's blood and by the word of their testimony, and they didn't love their lives until death" (Rev 12:11).

Your story is your anthem cry of God's glory, goodness, and grace to you. No one, not even the devil, can take that away from you. Declare it. Proclaim it. Storm the gates of hell with it. Don't give the devil a foothold. Stand on the promises of God and see Him finish your healing. His blood has already been shed. All that's left is the word of your testimony.

Rely on God's Sufficient Grace

God told Paul that His grace was sufficient for Paul to continue (2 Cor 12:9). We grapple with this passage because God did not heal Paul. He was giving Paul amazing revelations in heaven. I have always thought that God will use in exceedingly great ways those who suffer like Paul. The New Testament has a robust theology of suffering that we don't like to embrace.

Of course, no one should want to embrace suffering. We should not resign ourselves to suffering either. So, we are trying to walk the tightrope between embracing suffering and running from it. If you're like me, you try to understand why we must suffer in the first place.

I understand God uses suffering to further His Kingdom. Jesus suffered on the Cross, and the apostles and servants of God included a theology of suffering in their books. Your faith as you suffer, and yet trust God for healing and proclaim His name despite your current reality, inspires others and increases their faith.

Paul expected to suffer because he began as a persecutor of the Church. He speaks of equalizing his abuse of the Church with suffering as an apostle. What are we to make of this? Must we suffer for Christ to be His disciples? And if we must, do we all receive extra grace to suffer well?

Though Paul accepts God's answer that His grace is sufficient for him, he still calls it a "thorn in the flesh" and a "messenger of Satan." He did not say that *God* gave him this thorn in the flesh. When I woke up in the hospital and talked with my mom, I tried to stress to her that I believed my paralysis came from Satan, not God.

The New Testament has a robust theology of suffering that we don't like to embrace.

I don't know if we should embrace a theology of suffering for every believer. I don't want to elevate my situation and see that those who are on the enemy's hit list must go through great trials and suffering. I have noticed that many men and women who have great impact for God's Kingdom go through suffering and trials. They were not concerned about what God's ministry through them would be as they suffered. Most don't bring it up. Only after getting to know them, did I see what they went through. We shouldn't just accept suffering from our affliction either or think that this is how we should live from now on. Paul asked the Lord three times to remove this thorn (2 Cor 12:8).

Another powerful theology we find in Paul's writings is that God works His strength through our weaknesses (Rom 8:26; 2 Cor 12:10; 13:4). Jesus can use your affliction even though He did not give it to you. We must serve the Lord in our weakness so He is strong through us. This is why I find ways to minister to others despite my inability to continue in full-time ministry until the Lord's healing.

Thank Your Support Team

You didn't do this alone. You are walking through your affliction with the help of friends, prayer warriors, caregivers, and a host of others with similar conditions. Share your thanks with them so they can praise God with you.

Share your setbacks too so that they can pray for you. Include them in your life. Don't just do Facebook posts for sympathy. Let them *live life* with you. There's nothing better than celebrating with friends on your mountaintops, but it's important to ask for prayer and ministry from them when you are in your valleys, too.

For all they do for you and have ministered to you, you owe them gratitude. They minister to your various needs out of love, compassion, and a desire to serve the Lord. So, let them in on your life, and let them be ministering angels too. But don't forget to thank them profusely for their kindness to you.

Don't Give Up

Lastly, it's so easy to give up on your miracle healing. Our flesh wants to walk away from our situation. We don't want to talk to anyone. We don't want to pray about it. We don't want to keep on fighting. We don't want to inspire people or be faithful.

I get it. There are days when my nerve pain is so high because of the weather that I just want to moan and groan about it or give it the silent treatment. I can get snappy at people. I can push people away, even though I don't really mean to.

Yet we are mighty warriors in the spiritual realm. Jesus has made us conquerors and overcomers. See yourself with your spiritual armor. See yourself healed in the name of Jesus. Nothing can defeat you because you stand in the power of God.

If you don't see *yourself* that way, let God show you how *He* sees you. Let Him remind you of your identity in Him. He will pull back the curtain and invite the people you influence without your knowledge to tell you what a blessing you are. Let it happen—not to stroke your ego but to show you as He showed Elijah that you matter to others, you have influence and are effective, and without you they may not even know the Lord.

> **You matter to others, you have influence and are effective, and without you they may not even know the Lord.**

So, when you feel weak, you are strong, mighty with the power of the Lord behind you. Stand when you feel like curling up into a ball. Stand firm against the assault of the enemy. Beat back the darkness with the light of Jesus in you, and take on anything that stands between you and pressing forward to win the race and to know Jesus in His sufferings and His victory.

Let Me Pray for You

You are dealing with your affliction and other health issues related to it. Not everyone who interacts with you understands how to help. Some of them may not care as much as they should. More importantly, you may be losing hope and faith after many years of your affliction.

For all these needs and more, I understand some of them. No matter what you face, the Lord ministers to us perfectly. He understands because He has been there.

I want to pray for you ...

Heavenly Father, you know what your children are facing. You know how long we will have these afflictions. You have created us. You have intimate knowledge of our frame and being, and you care deeply for us. Thank you for the many blessings you lavish upon us. Be with us and bring us peace.

Lord Jesus, thank you for your goodness, comfort, and peace through our afflictions. You went to the Cross, suffered, and died to heal us from our afflictions. Give us your strength to deal with our afflictions until your complete healing. Heal us and relieve us of our pain. We look forward to celebrating our healing with you.

Holy Spirit, continue to be with us every day of this battle. Protect us and keep us. Comfort us in our pain. Remind us of the truth of Scripture. Walk with us as we wait on healing and teach us to wait expectantly on your timing.

In the name of the Father, the mighty name of the Son, and the comforting Holy Spirit, Amen.

Chapter 10
Minister to the Afflicted

"So the king will reply to them, saying, 'Truly I say to you, as you did to one of the least of these, my brothers, you did it to me.'"
(Matthew 25:40).

Many people don't know how to approach me. Or, once they do, they don't know what to say. Children are my favorite people because they have no filter. So many when they see me, look at their parent, and say, "What's wrong with him?" Even better are the parents surprised and horrified look. What do you say to a curious child about a man in a wheelchair with the weird, mangled-looking hand and tubes coming out of his neck?

For those of you who minister to the afflicted of all kinds, this is your chapter.

For those of you who minister to the afflicted of all kinds, this is your chapter. Realizing that people are caught off guard by my condition, I want to give you helps to minister to the afflicted effectively. I understand how you feel. What do you say and do for people with afflictions? How do you help them? Your heart is in the right place, but your head and hands may not know what to do.

I will speak of my condition, but the following pointers are useful no matter the affliction. Following these pointers, you will be ahead of the game. I've included a section on giving gifts to the afflicted. I mostly speak of my condition because it is extreme. If you can minister to me and quadriplegics, you can minister to most afflictions.

Honor the Wishes of the Afflicted

One of your biggest questions may be how to approach the afflicted. When people look at me, or they hear my vent go off and start beeping, it's quite a daunting effort to minister to me. People don't know what they can ask, how they can help, or even if I need their help.

I make myself as available as possible, but I am not every person with an affliction. Some people don't want to talk about their affliction. They don't want help, and they can have a nasty attitude. Consider a person's spiritual needs. Some are angry at God and the world. They don't take kindly to people wanting to help them.

Take the initiative to address the afflicted. Be prepared to be turned away. Don't take it personally. These may be hard to reach. If they don't want your help or input, don't give it. They may be working through spiritual and/or psychological PTSD. Their outward trauma may or may not be visible. No one can gauge the mental, spiritual, and relational shrapnel the afflicted suffer.

> No one can gauge the mental, spiritual, and relational shrapnel the afflicted suffer.

Above all, don't ignore them or treat them rudely. Treat the afflicted like you treat any other human being. When you come up to them, ask if you can pray for them. Don't give too much attention to their affliction. Ask, "Can I pray for you?" If they say yes, follow up with, "What can I pray for?" Just because their affliction is noticeable doesn't mean that is the top prayer request on their list.

My affliction is so obvious that most people want to pray for me to be healed. I welcome all prayers. Most of the time praying for my healing is my top prayer request, but the afflicted are not only concerned with their condition. Like you, they face the same problems in this world from financial hardship to other trials. Don't assume their prayer list is always the same thing.

Approach asking about their condition with caution. Ask them if it's OK to talk about their affliction. Some are OK with answering questions and open to discussion about their affliction. Others are much more guarded. Only go as far as the person is willing to go. Don't press any issues unless you know the person well. Sometimes an affliction will change the person's personality. They may have been open before their affliction but now feel closed off and guarded. Keep this in mind.

You Fulfill Jesus's Call

Jesus described compassion ministry when He talked about the final judgment with His disciples:

> For I was hungry, and you gave Me something to eat. I was thirsty, and you provided Me something to drink. I was a stranger, and you welcomed Me. I was naked and you clothed Me. I was sick, and you looked in on Me. I was in prison, and you came to Me. Then the righteous ones will answer him, saying, "Lord, when did we see you being hungry we fed you, or you were being thirsty, and we provided drink? And when did we see you as a stranger and we welcomed you, or naked and we provided clothing? And when did we see you being sick and in prison, and we came? So the king will reply to them, saying, "Truly I say to you, as you did to one of the least of these, my brothers, you did it to me." (Matt 25:35-40)

When you minister to the afflicted, you do a service to Jesus no matter how they respond to you. Everyone suffering an affliction goes through good and bad days, lesser and greater pain, and responds differently to you at different times. Even if they reject your ministry, Jesus sees your heart and willingness to help the afflicted.

Never be ashamed of trying to minister to them. Jesus calls us to offer compassion and service to those who need it. You fulfill Jesus's call even if you are rejected for trying. You offer a cup of cold water in their wilderness. If they reject you, that's on them. Don't feel ashamed if they don't accept your compassion.

I found that most people respond positively to prayer and to help. In the best situation, they will tell you what they need and how to help them. When people ask me if they can do anything, I tell them if I am in need. When they hear my vent beeping, I can tell they want to help. Unfortunately, most people don't know if I am in distress or if it is a common occurrence. I try to put them at ease.

Offer whatever service you can. If nothing else, pray silently to the Lord for them. If they have a specialized condition like I do, you can ask their caregiver if you can render assistance. If they don't have a caregiver, calmly wait to offer assistance by asking first if they need your help.

Wear the Shoes of the Afflicted

I know it's a cliché to tell people to walk a mile in the shoes of the afflicted, but it is important for you to think about their condition. Imagine you are a quadriplegic. You can't move anything. You rely on the kindness of others. I have nerve pain almost every day. Sometimes it is manageable, and other times it's not.

Any number of problems can arise, but the most common is my vent tubing disconnecting somewhere. Now I can't breathe. How would you feel if you could not breathe, were in pain most of the time, and had people standing around staring at you? Some afflicted people handle it better than others, but most of us don't like people staring at us. It's bad enough we are causing a ruckus.

Be mindful of a person's condition. How would you feel if you were them? Try to think of what their condition practically causes in their body. What unusual circumstances do they face? How would you react to the same condition? I've been a quadriplegic for nine years. If I don't look worried, whatever is happening to me has happened before.

Look at the face of the afflicted when they are dealing with an episode related to their condition. Do they look like they are in distress? If not, don't look too worried. When you can put yourself in the shoes of the afflicted, try to experience what they experience; it will make you a much better servant for the Lord. If they are open to questions, ask about their condition and what they go through every day.

When I was in nursing homes, most nurses, CNAs, and respiratory therapists were naturally compassionate. Whatever service they gave me, they tried the best they knew how to help me. Occasionally, there were people who did not consider how to compassionately assist me. They could do more harm than good.

When you minister to the afflicted as a caregiver, be gentle at first. Ask questions about how you are serving the afflicted. Let them guide you in their care. If they are unable to communicate, continue to be gentle in your assistance.

The Holy Spirit helps us when we minister to the afflicted. When we ask Him what to do or how to serve others, He gives us the courage to reach out, the kindness to serve, and the wisdom to help the afflicted. Rely on His cues as you serve others.

Give the Gift of Yourself

Many people with afflictions are very lonely. Because most people don't know how to help them, the afflicted often suffer loneliness. You can offer yourself as a friendly face, a calm voice in the raging storm. When you are with the afflicted, be present in the moment. Offer yourself kindly. Be with them. Be attentive and open. Be gentle.

Don't put on a brave face. Don't be someone you're not. Be real and genuine. Treat them like you would treat anyone else. They need a friend. They need you. We don't realize what a gift our presence can be to someone. Be genuine. Don't try to fix everything. Just be present, and you will provide one of greatest gifts to the afflicted.

Serving the afflicted is a gift they cannot return. You serve and honor Jesus as you minister to the afflicted. You represent Jesus well. If they cannot direct you, do things for them they cannot do themselves. It's a blessing to me when someone can help me with something I cannot do. I believe that serving the afflicted has a special reward in heaven for those who serve without complaining and who compassionately offer themselves.

Speak and Pray in Faith

When you spend time with the afflicted, make it productive. I don't mean getting a lot of things done. Productive time can mean different things in different situations. Sometimes the most productive thing you can do is to sit at the bedside of the afflicted and enjoy one another's company.

Other times, productive time means praying, talking, and enjoying fellowship. In every situation, though, you can be productive by turning to spiritual matters. This begins with knowing the spiritual background of the afflicted person. Are they a believer? Are they open to talking about Jesus? You will never have a more eternally impactful relationship than one that includes Jesus.

If the person is uninterested in Jesus, talk about healing. I can't imagine anyone with an affliction who likes having it. Follow steps already mentioned, like asking to pray for them. If the afflicted person is a believer, there is much to do that makes your time together productive for the Kingdom.

When you speak about faith and healing, speak with faith. Don't doubt the power of the Lord or that He can minister to the afflicted through you. This is not positive thinking or positive speaking. You can believe that God will answer your prayers and honor your speech for healing.

Read the Bible with the afflicted. Talk about what you read. Read healing stories from the Bible that are similar to their affliction. Let the Word of God encourage and minister to the person. Work through a list of healing Scriptures together. Ask the afflicted what their favorite passages are in the Bible. Pray over the healing Scriptures and declare them over the afflicted person.

You should not psychoanalyze your prayers or their results. Just be faithful to pray and believe. Let God do the rest.

As you pray for the afflicted, pray in faith for healing results. Pray specifically to your expectations. If you only have enough faith to see incremental improvements, pray that away. Why not ask big things from a big God? I like to say I'm going for the gold. I want complete healing. I am even praying that God heals my eyes along with the rest of my body.

You don't have to only pray about healing. The afflicted person may have other needs. Much Christian conversation about healing and prayer revolves around problematic teaching. For instance, Jesus did not always rely on the faith of the afflicted to do miracles. Sometimes faith came from those around the afflicted person. The Gospels credit the four friends who bring the paralytic man to Jesus with faith to see him healed (Mark 2:5).

Jesus only requires that you pray in faith, not doubting His power to answer your prayer and heal the afflicted. There are no clear-cut reasons why people are not healed when you pray for them. You should not psychoanalyze your prayers or their results. Just be faithful to pray and believe. Let God do the rest.

Agree with the afflicted in faith-filled prayers. The Bible teaches that agreement in prayer is powerful (Matt 18:18-20). Do not blame the afflicted person if they are not healed after your prayer. During your prayer, ask the afflicted person if there are any changes. This is biblical because Jesus did it when He asked the blind man if he could see (Mark 8:23-25). When the man could only see men as trees walking, Jesus prayed again.

Only in rare circumstances, and if the afflicted person can handle it, should you pray for long periods of time. Some afflictions cause weakness of the body or extreme fatigue. Be mindful of the person you pray for. Long prayers and extended prayer times do not necessarily yield greater results. Jesus taught us not to pray empty-worded prayers. Be purposeful in your prayer.

Avoid Christian slogans and clichés.

You don't have to pray with formulas. If you find a written prayer applicable to the afflicted person, then there's nothing wrong with using that. You can make it a springboard into spontaneous prayer.

Let it boost faith in God's healing power. Pray for the afflicted with the prayer of faith, and do not doubt as you pray (Jas 5:14-16).

A few cautions are in order as you speak with and pray for the afflicted. First, avoid Christian slogans and clichés. These are not helpful and can discourage the afflicted. Slogans and clichés gloss over the reality of their situation. They sound hollow in the face of the afflicted person's current reality. They don't help solve problems. You mean well, but the clichés do not.

It is better to empathize with the afflicted person and admit that you don't always understand how they feel. As much as you try to put yourself in their shoes, you also don't want to act like you completely understand. Acknowledge that you can't completely empathize with them but are trying. Provide a listening ear. Develop good active listening skills.

When you pray, do not pray, "Lord, if it's your will ..." The Bible teaches that healing is always God's will. You can declare the healing promises of God over the afflicted person instead. Customize your prayer according to the affliction and conversation you have had with the person. Always allow the Holy Spirit to speak through you and to minister to the person.

Encourage and build up the afflicted person as you visit. Speak God's truth to their situation. If they are discouraged or losing hope, challenge their faith with Scripture. Remind them of God's blessings. Understand what they are feeling but do what you can to build their hope and faith up. Don't give up on them—and don't let them give up on God.

Be faithful to visit the person and spend quality time with them. I look forward to visitors. If they continually change meeting times or don't come when they said they would, it can feel discouraging. Afflicted people may not have much interaction with the outside world. Life happens, but don't make a habit of changing meeting times. God will reward you for your time and effort.

Be Jesus with Skin On

It may surprise you how you can minister to a person without realizing it. When I was in the nursing home, to this day I remember Yolanda. She volunteered in the cafeteria. I received meals in my room because I could not make it to the dining room to eat. She came to my room every morning, read a devotional and some Scripture to me.

She took time out of her busy schedule to minister to me more than she will ever know. Ministering to the afflicted may come naturally for you, or maybe you have to intentionally work at it. Realize you can be Jesus to the afflicted. Putting forth an effort to minister to them means the world.

Don't underestimate your effect on them. They will not forget you. Being Jesus with skin on means that you minister to their needs and have compassion on them. It doesn't mean you are perfect or an expert at compassion ministry. It only means you do your best to see the person and step out to offer yourself in genuine friendship.

Give Mindful, Useful Gifts

Before I began writing this book, I reached out to my social media community and asked what they wanted to know about me, or what would help them in this book. One person, caught off guard, asking me what gifts are appropriate for quadriplegics. She ministered to a quadriplegic for years but never knew what to get them for a gift.

First, people say it's the thought that counts. With some afflictions, limitations mean that you must be even more thoughtful. What could they use that nobody has thought to get them? If you minister to them for a while, you might pick up on what they say, or what you think they could use.

Second, gifts for the afflicted are usually practical. They can solve a problem or grant added independence and mobility to the person. Sometimes the best gift you can give is a gift card or money for the person to use. It depends on the situation and the person. Refrain from just asking a person what they want. If you cannot think of anything, then you can ask.

So, what do you get a quadriplegic? I cannot use my hands. Some quadriplegics cannot talk or communicate well. It may be one of the most challenging afflictions that you may ever come across. Short of coming up with a new way to get past the spinal cord injury causing paralysis, here are some of the gifts I have received.

For Christmas and my birthday, I often get Amazon gift cards. These are useful because I can get what I need, and I have access to the Internet. Family and friends have gotten large blankets to drape over my body to calm my nerves. It's amazing how well they relieve much of my nerve pain.

They also get me hot sauces and spicy peppers. I like spicy food. The hotter the better. See if there is a food item or type of food the afflicted person likes. Perhaps they are a coffee or tea connoisseur. Keep in mind that some people with extreme conditions do not eat but have a feeding tube.

Although people have not bought me Amazon echoes, these are an exceptional item for paralyzed people. Coupled with Wi-Fi plugs and switches, compatible devices, and other technologies, they provide much more than a tech toy. They have given me independence to control lights, fans, TVs, playing music, trivia games, set reminders and alarms, and do a host of other activities. This item facilitates independence and helps me assert some control over my situation. Some people are not tech savvy, but even for them these devices can be helpful. The greatest gift I received in the nursing home was from a friend with whom I share an affinity for writing. He bought Dragon NaturallySpeaking speech-to-text and software so I could write books with my voice.

I don't think he realized Dragon has much more versatility than writing. I use it to control my computer and every program I have. I can move the mouse, use shortcut keyboard commands, and it gives me complete independence and autonomy.

I can even play some games with it. When I was in the nursing home, I had nothing to do. Operating my computer allowed me to talk to people online and on the phone, be part of online society again, and write sermons and Bible studies. It gave me purpose again.

My friend who gave me the gift of Dragon will never realize its lasting effects and the independence it gives me. Dragon is not an inexpensive purchase, but if you have a quadriplegic friend who is good with computers and tech, it's another great gift idea. There may be a less expensive option that does the same, but in my opinion it is the best speech-to-text software available.

Another gift perfect for me is books. I prefer electronic books (ebooks) and audiobooks because I cannot turn pages. I am a bibliophile. Seriously, I have a disease. I buy and read books 24/7. I'm pretty sure I need counseling because of it.

As with the rest of the counsel of this chapter, these are only suggestions. You must customize the gifts you choose to give with the needs of the afflicted person to whom you minister. You must also customize your ministry to their affliction and needs. You may find other people or resources to help you minister more effectively to the afflicted person's needs. Ask people who take care of them. Try to think what you would find useful as a gift if you were in their shoes.

Let Me Pray for You

As I prayed for afflicted people in the last chapter, I want to lift up before the Lord the request that your ministry to an afflicted person be most effective.

Heavenly Father, thank you for people who step out in faith and follow your lead to minister to the afflicted. Bless them beyond measure. Pour out your love and compassion through them. Help them to know what to say and do for those to whom they minister.

Jesus, I bring this beautiful, kind, thoughtful minister of your grace before you. Bless them for their ministry. Let them know how much of a difference they are making in the lives of the afflicted. Bless their efforts. Give them creative solutions in their ministry to the afflicted.

Holy Spirit, minister in and through these wonderful servants. Give them insight into how to minister to others. Speak through them, empower them, and anoint them to serve. Give them the gifts they need to be effective. Lead and direct their path. Reward their boldness and courage to step out in faith.

In the mighty name of our Lord Jesus Christ, Amen.

Dear Reader

Thank you for taking the time to read my book. I appreciate your support and hope that it helps you to believe God's promises for your healing. May we all seek the Lord for the healing of our bodies and see our faith transform our reality to wholeness.

There's another way you could continue to support me. One or more of these actions will give the book more visibility or connect you to everything I'm doing:

- Please leave a review. If you go to the place you bought the book and leave a review, whether good or bad, this helps the book to be more visible in the marketplaces. This is a quick way to support both this book and my ministry.
- Please sign up for my email list. If you are interested in following me or engaging with me more, you can go to my blog at www.Jonathansrock.com and sign up to my website. You'll get a free gift and be emailed anytime I release a blog or news.
- Please like my Facebook author page and share my books and posts. Type "Author Jonathan Srock" in the Facebook search box. You'll get even more news about my activities. Also, you can share this book and more of my resources in your social media feed.

You can always contact me through my blog at www.Jonathansrock.com or my email address (srockenator@Gmail.com). I hope to hear from you!

Blessing,

Jonathan Srock

About the Author

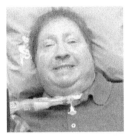

Rev. Jonathan Srock has been an ordained minister with the Assemblies of God since 2010. He received two bachelor's degrees in Biblical Languages and Pastoral Ministries, as well as a Master of Divinity from the Assemblies of God Theological Seminary.

Jonathan was privileged to serve as the Lead Pastor of New Life Assembly in Shillington, PA for five years before suffering sudden paralysis in 2013. He is part of the PennDel Ministry Network.

A Christian since 1988, Jonathan is a quadriplegic and lives in Central Pennsylvania with his parents. He enjoys preaching in local churches, writing books, blogging, and answering questions about God and the Bible. His passion is to imprint the character of Christ through teaching and preaching God's Word. Losing control of his body has not dissuaded him from teaching and preaching. He loves to preach in churches that invite him to share biblical preaching and teaching.

Jonathan spends his time blogging at JonathanSrock.com, writing books and devotionals, and preparing sermons and sharing Bible studies. The other great love of his life is creative writing. Jonathan enjoys writing articles about God and the Bible, and any other subject he researches in Christianity. He also writes nonfiction books on various Christian subjects. His favorite writing challenges include short stories and fiction works in science fiction and retelling Bible stories in a fresh way. He also enjoys reading, watching sports, and geeking out over computers in his "spare" time.